THIS FREEDOM

THIRTEEN NEW RADIO PLAYS

THIS FREEDOM

THIRTEEN NEW RADIO PLAYS

BY ARCH OBOLER

WITH A FOREWORD BY ROBERT J. LANDRY

AND NOTES ON ACTING AND PRODUCTION

BY ARCH OBOLER

RANDOM HOUSE · NEW YORK

FIRST PRINTING

COPYRIGHT, 1942, BY RANDOM HOUSE, INC.

PUBLISHED SIMULTANEOUSLY IN CANADA BY
THE MACMILLAN COMPANY OF CANADA, LIMITED

MANUFACTURED IN THE UNITED STATES OF AMERICA

TO
ELEANOR

FOREWORD

By ROBERT J. LANDRY

Radio Critic and Radio Editor *Variety*

During the first half of a history just over twenty years old, the leadership of American radio broadcasting was necessarily preoccupied with the conquest of static, the perfection of the engineering aspects of transmission and reception, the marketing of millions of sets, the organizing of stations and networks and with simple, makeshift program services. In its early days, radio was compelled—for purposes of survival—to persuade people generally, and skeptical businessmen particularly, that privately financed radio was here to stay, an integrated part of modern life, a plausible advertising medium.

We need not laboriously detail radio management's many steps, the innumerable and vexatious problems of engineer, salesman, statistician and entrepreneur. At any rate, the pace of development was sensational. Nearly everyone has been impressed, first, by the mechanical marvel itself and then by the brilliant organization of a vast industry based upon it.

We now enter upon a more reflective, more mature, more socially responsible period of broadcasting. Today the writer and the director are coming into their own. Evidence of this fact is the appearance of books such as this, bringing between boards some of the scripts that previously lived and died in mimeograph. We need not be self-consciously "arty" to appreciate the challenge of radio, far beyond soap and toothpaste and cigarettes, in the realm of ideas and morals and morale.

FOREWORD

Already there is evidence of rising levels of discrimination as regards radio music, radio advertising-copy and radio comedians' jokes. Not unnaturally, serious radio drama, somewhat behind the noisier shows, has also benefited from the criticism-encouraging forces of time.

We have heard enough to realize that the serious dramatic radio form can clarify and vivify certain ideas and theses important to our democracy and our liberties which are not easily conveyed by direct speechifying; enough to realize that radio drama can evoke emotional responses and provide spiritual experiences of an intensity comparable to the most effective productions of stage and screen.

Arch Oboler has explored and enriched the possibilities of radio drama. He has not been abashed by the smiles or the awful indifference of those whose slothful motto is "so what?" He has not exploited the radio medium solely as an easy way to make a living. When he has fallen short, it has not been for lack of trying, and his best efforts have been formidable blows against trite themes and devices.

As with most radio dramas, the plays in this volume are written to be heard rather than read, and the reader must always be aware of this. Yet they deserve the permanence afforded by book publication, since they formulate new technics and mark an advance in the development of radio play-writing.

Only superficially, I think, is radio drama a stripped-down, concentrated, one-dimensional, aural version of stage drama. Instead of saying that radio precludes scenery, props, make-up and lights, it would be closer to critical focus to say that the stage precludes a nation-wide audience. The true importance and challenge of radio drama, as of radio generally, reposes in its unique, unduplicated capacity of creating for the first time in history a near-universal audience. (Even radio "flops" may measure their audiences by the millions.) Statisticians assure us that for particular programs or for especial occasions, 30,000,000 to 50,000,000 persons, or more, may be simultaneously exposed to a voice, a personality, an idea, a mood, a soul, a body of information—or, if you wish to state it negatively for the dictators—a lie, a demeaning spirit, a polluted stream.

I think it is a sense of these dimensions implicit in radio, and only dimly exploited by radio drama to date, that keeps Arch Oboler chronically excited.

CONTENTS

NOTES ON ACTING AND PRODUCTION

By Arch Oboler

You are supposed to wait until you're dead. Then, out of a trunk, or out of a hat, or from under an old desiccated lover, they pull a lifetime accumulation of notes, and someone who disliked you a great deal puts the notes together and everything that you felt personally about your own work is hung up like the wash.

I think I'm alive. For the moment, at least, the sky is clear of Stuka bombers. And the possibilities of either accumulated notes or desiccated lovers are quite remote, so let's talk about what I thought while writing these radio plays and producing them and actually putting them on the air. I believe it's just as interesting to know why a man wrote a play as to read the play. Did he write it because the bank told him his check balance was getting lower than the third vice-president's jowls? And what happened during the first production? Did every plot involution and dialogue twist go as is, or was a little on-the-job carpentry done? Oh, yes—and why was he so insistent upon that particular leading lady?

All right, you're asking—and I'll tell you. I'll tell you about geniuses and glandular Hollywood stars, and how to own two swimming pools through one dictaphone, and all about radio critics who hate radio, and what she said to me just before she closed the bedroom door. Hidden among all this will be a few plays to each of which an average of ten million people have listened. I mention the number of listeners only because if these were vest-pocket dramas I'd feel compunctions about surrounding them with the whys, whens and where-fores. But so many human beings and critics have said in so many words, "Oboler, why and how do you get that way?" that I feel no qualms about being the first radio playwright publicly to remove his artistic trousers.

Words to an Actor

You say you like radio acting. You say the thought of standing in front of a microphone and addressing a million-plus audience is an excitement that you want to know about. All right, I'll tell you about it.

Of Performance

When radio was quite young, one of its wonders was the uniformly horrible performances turned in by stars of stage and screen when they appeared for the first time before a microphone. Could it be, the whisper went around wherever it is that whispers go around, that our wonder boys and girls had artistic feet of clay?

But the years of the kilocycles went on and the performances of the stars gradually began to improve, because most of them, largely through accident, discovered that, as NBC's C. L. Menser says, radio is a thing of intimacy.

In other words, where the very mechanics of the theatre make it necessary to project one's voice sufficiently to be heard in the last row, in the medium of radio every listener is standing right before the actor and there must be an under-emphasis in both the coloring and the projection of the speech.

So there, in a vitamined, fortified-chocolate capsule, is the basic prerogative of acting for the radio medium: the continued recognition of the fact that one is performing in an intimate medium to an audience of one whose loud-speaker is as close to you as you are to the microphone.

Of Mechanics

One of the most successful radio actors I know isn't a very good actor. I mean to say that, within the man, there isn't that meeting of emotion and mentality which results in a stirring performance.

And yet directors keep the man busy for the simple reason that they can always depend on him to give a broadcast performance which brings out the best of what he has learned during rehearsals.

How does he do it? He doesn't depend on inspiration. He doesn't depend on memory. He marks his scripts.

He Marks His Scripts

The definite indication of an amateur actor, to a director, is to see a script-page which, after hours of rehearsal, is as free of notations as a blank check.

Every possible marking should be used as a sign-post to a good performance.

By that I don't mean long philosophical notations on the margins; I refer to the underlining of words for emphasis, the use of lines to indicate pauses and breathing spaces, and other scribbled short-hand interpolations to enable one, at a glance, to anticipate change of pace and change of mood.

A good memory is the leaning-post of the stage actor; a good pencil is the bulwark of the radio performer against the uncertainties of inspiration at the time of actual broadcast.

Of Auditions

You met the man. He said, "Be at the studio at 10 and I will listen to you." And now it is 10 o'clock. You are standing in front of a tin box with holes in it which, they tell you, is a mike. Beyond you, in a surrealistic blur, you see various individuals in a control-room staring out at you.

And so you begin to talk into the microphone, giving like Hayes or Cornell or Evans or Lunt.

But you really don't know anything about microphone technics. When you start talking very loudly, you see a look of horror come over the face of the man behind the controls, and when you speak softly, arms wave madly behind that glass, motioning you heaven knows where, in or out or up—or down through the floor, where your heart is.

So let us, for a moment, talk of microphone technics. No matter what the phony "Get-on-the-radio-in-ten-easy-lessons" schools tell you, it's all quite simple. When you speak loudly, you step away from the microphone. When you speak softly, you come in closer. When you are supposed to be leaving a scene, you speak as you walk away from the microphone. If the fade is to be abrupt, you turn your head away as you speak and as you walk, or else you walk sideways away from the microphone instead of backward, since most microphones cut off sharply when one moves from them on a parallel line to the face of the microphone.

Of course, there are other simple little microphone tricks which one learns through experience, such as coming to within

xvi

eight or ten inches of the microphone and speaking very softly when one wishes to indicate an extremely intimate tone, or turning one's head away from the microphone when the action calls for a sudden extremely loud tone—but the basics are simply a matter of working about two feet away from the microphone and speaking directly into it in ordinary scenes—stepping in to within a foot of the microphone in intimate scenes, and turning one's head or taking a long step backward when there is to be a great deal of voice used.

So now, as you audition, your microphonic behavior is thoroughly professional; no one in the control room could possibly know that your knees are castanets.

But—what are the words you are saying? What material are you using to win that director and influence that production manager? Is it something so familiar that the man, at the first few words, has mentally shut his ears?

Yet another question: are you doing something that you have the ability to do, or have you wish-thought yourself into reading a piece of material completely unsuited for anything but ego-inflation?

And a last question: is the material that you are speaking something which you have picked out as being of interest to that particular director? In other words, if that very important little man in the control-room directs nothing but very corn-fed mystery stories, are you giving him something which his equally corn-fed mind can understand, or are you trying to overpower him with O'Neill?

To recapitulate the entire situation in a few words: choose material which is not too familiar; choose material which is honestly within the range of your abilities; choose material which will be of interest to the particular person who is listening to your audition.

You ask where to get such material? Well, I don't mind if you use a short cutting from any of these plays of mine; furthermore, the newspapers and magazines are full of good short bits which, although not in the radio form, are excellent for the short audition time which the average director will give you to prove that you are a better man or woman than Orson Hayes.

And, to the women, a last word: don't open your audition by reading something which runs the gamut of emotions, including rape, revolution, Anna Christie, and Camille—all within five minutes.

Choose something simple, and not too emotional.

The poor director, expecting the usual barrage of tears and breast-beating, will prick up his ears at your good taste and will think you are so wonderful that he will immediately put you into the lead of his next opus and, before you can say "ten percent," you will be in a swimming pool in Hollywood with Victor Mature.

Of Persistence

But—may I come in very close to the microphone as I prescribed before and whisper this?—you may audition, and nothing may happen.

Well, what of it? If you're any good at all at what you want to do, here is the place for a very necessary little demon of persistency to start his operations.

Yes, persistency—the continual pounding and beating at doors and at other people that will, blitzkriegs permitting, get you the measure of success that your ability or your personality warrants.

How to be persistent with directors and producers? I

shouldn't answer this. It means that the directors' union will turn my picture to the wall.

Persistence means calling on advertising agencies, and sitting in waiting rooms, and telephoning the men who put programs together, and sending them letters, and every other ways and means you can devise to keep you and your name and abilities in the directorial eye.

You will be made very unhappy at times. Directors, in self-defense, will look through you as you talk. Some of them may even tell you to go away and bury your lovely head.

But, eventually, if you have ability or a face prettier than the norm, you will find yourself standing in front of a microphone, awaiting that very tense but very exciting moment when a director will point a finger at you and you know you are on the air.

THE ART OF PEACEFUL PRODUCTION

I know that there is a school of thought which feels that great productions result only if the leading lady becomes hysterical, the supporting cast hates each other virulently, and the studio by broadcast time resembles an emotional blitzkrieg.

I believe that there should be some semblance of maturity inside of the control room. If fist-beating and arm-flinging is necessary, it should be used for that all-encompassing purpose: a mechanically clean, well-interpreted broadcast play.

NOTES ON ACTING AND PRODUCTION

Of Function

Too many production men use the broadcast studio to inflate their aching egos. I believe that the function of a production man is to take the author's script and bring it to the air in the most effective manner possible. That's an objective job which doesn't necessarily include impressing the unfortunate cast with one's own importance, or with using said cast as a whipping-boy because one has had an unfortunate creative, sex, or financial life.

No plan, no objectivity, can make a good play out of a poor one, and the director who thinks he can do so is too good for this world.

But the director with ability can, by under-emphasis and artful cutting and rearranging, remove some of the odor of the unfortunate drama and, by doing so, give it some semblance of reason and reality.

Of Planning

I have long felt that the production man who, given a normal amount of rehearsal time, has a sloppy broadcast with indeterminate characterizations, mixed cues, badly timed sound effects and wrong sound levels, should be hung by the neck vertically from the nearest horizontal antenna.

A good production happens invariably when the production man plans his rehearsal. The inspiration type of producer—the one who dashes in, sets eyes on the sound table, ignores the waiting cast and spends an hour getting the exact effect of a heavy fog in Istanbul, then suddenly recalls the actors and jumps into a furious rehearsal of lines, until suddenly he breaks off to try out a musical cue, all without conscious se-

quence or continuity—this sort of director is the basic cause
for the ulcerous condition of actors' stomachs and the cancer-
ous condition of listeners' ears.

Plan—plan—plan—the director must know exactly where
he is going and exactly how much time he can spend on each
element of the rehearsal, otherwise, one fine day he is going
to look up at the clock and discover that he has three minutes before air-time in which to rehearse a dozen unrehearsed
matters—and that moment will be the genesis of the "nervous
breakdown" item which will eventually appear in his home-
town paper.

The basic elements of any dramatic production are:

1. Cast readings of script off and on microphone.
2. Sound rehearsal without and then with cast.
3. Music rehearsal.
4. Dress rehearsal where words and sound and music are
   finally co-ordinated.
5. The actual broadcast.

Taking these elements and dividing up the given rehearsal
time among them may sound very elementary, but it is the
only path to peaceful production.

Of Casts

Perhaps you are allergic to goldenrod or to rabbits' fur or
to buck-teethed brunettes.

My own private allergy happens to be to directors who
think that actors should be treated as full-fledged cretins.

I believe that a group of actors have to be treated with the
same delicacy or subtlety or vigor or circumlocution or hon-
esty or deviousness as a similar group of, say, sewing-machine

salesmen or motion-picture producers, or juke-box operators, or utility magnates.

He who enters the studio and charges through his actors, swinging a broad-edged sword, is not only a fool but an infant, for only the very immature do not know that human beings, in spite of their mass sameness, have to be dealt with as individuals.

There is one sure way of getting type readings, corny characterizations, or whatever your own favorite wording of acting clichés happens to be. That way is to hand the cast their scripts, group them around a microphone, and tell them to go ahead and be terrific.

The actor, even the best of them, knowing practically nothing about the author's intent, will look for a face-saving exit, and that will be through this sort of a mental track-meet: "Irish character, eh? Let me think. I'll play this the way I did that Irishman three weeks ago in that godawful 'The Adventures of Sadie' script I did for the Sexy Soap Hour."

And when the author listens in to the broadcast and hears what happened to his soulful Irish character, he turns to his friends with the look of a doeless deer and pleads, "But I didn't write *that!*"

The sane way, then, to get meaningful characterizations is to keep the microphone away from the cast until they have had time to get both the author's and the director's plot and characterization ideas, and, above all, have had time to do a little analysis of their own.

Of Sound Rehearsal

Sound-rehearsal preliminaries should be held without the cast; it is virtually impossible to hear sound effects objectively when actors are saying the words in their scripts.

After the sound is set basically, that is, after one has chosen the particular recordings or manual sound-effects which are best for the purpose, then is the time to co-ordinate them with the dialogue.

Above all, sound should never be used for itself, but only as an integral part of the story. And cute devices and trick devices should be viewed and listened to with as suspicious a directorial eye and ear as a government accountant checking your last year's tax report.

Of Music Rehearsal

Here again pre-cast rehearsals are great sanity-savers. Whether the musical background is to be a handful of recordings, or an organist, or Mr. Toscanini, time spent checking the cues without cast or sound is time prudently spent.

After the orchestra knows the notes and the routining of cues it is time enough to open the doors to the rest of the company.

Of Dress Rehearsals

The production man who says "Dress rehearsals? Never bother with them!" is admitting that he allocates his rehearsals so badly that he never finds time for a proper final smoothing of rough edges. For that is what the dress rehearsal is: a last-chance polishing job to luster up dull spots before the broadcast.

The scheduling of this final run-through should be such that there is at least half an hour left in which the actors can renew their energies.

If the dress rehearsal is running dangerously close to air-time, and the production man discovers that the actors are "giving their all," he should break into the rehearsal and thus prevent the draining of energies which should be saved for actual broadcast.

The production man who rehearses right up to the moment the red "you're-on-the-air" sign flashes, finds, in many instances, that all the spontaneity has gone into the rehearsal, and nothing is left for the actual performance.

And that, believe me, is an unhappy situation to find oneself in the middle of, particularly if there is no cyanide within reach!

Of Broadcasts

And so we have the sequence of peaceful productions: A certain number of hours with cast alone, a certain amount of time with sound alone, a certain amount with music alone, then the joining together of these elements by first combining cast and sound, then cast and music, and the culmination in a critical run-through of the dress rehearsal.

Above all, by air-time, the director's script should have become a blueprint of the production. It should be so marked before and during the rehearsals that, by simply following his own sign-posts, the director cannot go wrong in timing or in cueing engineer, actors, sound men, or musicians.

One plan is to mark cues in vari-colored pencil: cues to the cast in red, cues to sound in blue, and those to the orchestra leader or organist in black.

If a one-color pencil is used, some production men circle the cast cues, put a triangle around the sound cues, and a wavy line around music cues; whatever means of identification are made use of, marking the script in great detail pre-broadcast makes for clean mechanics during the tenseness of the actual performance.

And now, my friend, you're on the air. You sit in the control-room, eyes on script, and, through the monitor loud-speaker, the words and the sound and the music are coming to you as they are to the relatives of the cast listening in Cicero, and New Rochelle, and Azusa.

And you haven't a thing to do now. Not a thing. Other than to pray that the weak-standed microphone won't collapse, and to importune the Deity that Sound won't mix any of the recordings, and to entreat the Fates that your leading lady won't turn over two pages instead of one and so lose her place, and to implore the gods that the news-room won't break in with a special news-flash, and to supplicate the Stars that none of the engineers upstairs will sleepily throw the wrong switch when you ask for an echo-chamber, and to appeal to the All Highest that the crazy cymbalist doesn't drop his cymbal while the woman is dying, and to petition with Paternosters that your first-time-on-the-air leading man doesn't pass out, and to bequest the Most Benign that your timing was right, otherwise the play will be cut off the air during the final scene, and without the final scene it isn't an understandable play, and to implore the Universe that no one drops a page, or jumps a cue, or trips over anything, or mistakes his cue for someone else's, or talks too fast, or talks too slow, or forgets the last-minute cut in the script, or foozles a line, or faints, or dies.

That's all!

SUFFER LITTLE CHILDREN

It was just before the Second World War. The English and French Fat-Bottoms had decided that they could buy "peace in our time" from the fascist gangsters; thousands of German and Austrian children knew the terror of the "new order"— of brutality.

In America, the Quakers, ever ready to stand in the way of man's inhumanity to man, went to Congress in an effort to get a bill passed that would permit these pitiful children to find temporary refuge in the homes of hundreds of American families who expressed a desire to play the part of foster parents to these German Catholic, Jewish and Protestant children whose parents were begging that their children be taken away from Mr. Shickelgruber's Chamber of Horrors.

Senator Wagner introduced the measure, and then, to the amazement of every decent-minded American, ax-grinding politicians and axis-inspired pressure groups, together with moronic pseudo-patriotic persons, jumped on the bill with multitudinous feet.

The Friends Society came to me; they asked me to do a radio program that would tell the story of these refugee children. The broadcast would originate from Washington before an invited audience. They went on to say that in whatever I wrote, Katharine Hepburn would play the lead; she would come by plane from New York, where she was playing in Philadelphia Story. *Between her histrionic abilities and my words the weight on the scales would be shifted, and the most rabid "Keep America Safe from the Brats" would see the*

2

error of their ways, and the little refugees would escape the torments of the new concentration-camp civilization.

I was very tired. I had been writing and casting a play every week for almost a year. And New York City was hotter than a Congressman. So I sat down with those parts of the Congressional Record *which concern themselves with the public hearings on this refugee-children bill. I wanted to read objectively, but within a few pages my objectivity sizzled with the heat of anger.*

> *"These children will grow up and will be added to the ranks of the unemployed!"*
>
> *"Let each nation take care of its own!"*
>
> *"We have enough foreign elements in our country!"*
>
> *"America for Americans!"*
>
> *"Let's mind our own business!"*

All the pressure groups were there on record fighting to prevent a few hundred children, ranging in ages from babes-in-arms to the ripe age of 14, from destroying (they said) the economic equilibrium of our struggling democracy. Oh, there was no doubt of it, according to the words they put into the Congressional Record—*open the immigration gates to these babies and our way of life was doomed.*

A nation with a surplus of land and food denying temporary shelter to babies!

And the loudest "Don't let them in" came from women!

I was sorry the Congressional Record *didn't have pictures. I wanted to see the sort of women who had stood up and said the plight of these children was not our concern. I wanted to see the flat-chested, secretionless psychopaths, those paragons of immorality.*

For, the more I read, the more I believed that theirs was a

3

great immorality, a definite evidence of a slackening of basic moralities among the "righteous" people.

Economics, when the fate of children is at stake?

Politics over the happiness of babies?

My typewriter damned them, but when I was through damning, I tore up the play and took a deep breath. No—screaming the iniquity of it all wouldn't help the American Friends in their pitiful crusade for the obvious; we'd have to sneak up on these Congressmen, twist their viscera with simple emotions.

So I wrote Suffer Little Children *and, on a very hot day in a very hot Washington hotel ballroom before an audience of about five thousand very hot Washingtonians, we broadcast hopefully. The visible audience wept unashamedly.*

But our subversive labors were in vain. Senator Wagner's bill was defeated, Mr. Shickelgruber kept his embryo slave labor, and the dumb division in our democracy triumphed!

SUFFER LITTLE CHILDREN

ANNOUNCER. The scene: A great luxury liner returning from Europe to America.

(*Sound: Hoot of ship, back.*)

ANNOUNCER. It is late at night.

(*Sound: Fade-in sigh of wind, continue behind.*)

ANNOUNCER. A girl stands on the boat deck looking out into the darkness, her face to the wind that lifts white-caps on the tumbling sea. Suddenly, an older woman approaches and speaks.

(*Sound: Wind sighs.*)

AUNT (*fade-in*). Well, Ronnie, I must say this is a peculiar way to behave!

RONNIE (*indifferently*). What did you say, Aunt Mary?

AUNT. I said it distinctly, and you heard me! A very peculiar way to behave, particularly your last night on shipboard! Do you realize that people have been asking about you?

RONNIE. Have they?

AUNT. The Stevensons were quite upset, and I assure you I had quite a time explaining to the captain! I couldn't for the life of me understand what happened to you!

(*Sound: Wind sighs.*)

AUNT. Ronnie, did you hear what I said?

RONNIE. Yes. . . . I heard. . . .

AUNT. Well?

RONNIE. I'm quite all right. . . .

AUNT. Then come downstairs! Standing up here in the cold. . . .

RONNIE. Please—I'm all right. . . .

AUNT. Good heavens! I hadn't noticed! You're still wearing a skirt and sweater. Ronnie, what *is* the matter with you? (*Sound: Wind sighs.*)

RONNIE. Four—people . . .

AUNT. People? Oh, that! Well, after all, my dear, there are always a certain number of undesirables on board a ship this size. And if you'd only stop wandering up and down the second and third classes you'd find everything quite right and proper!

RONNIE (*repeats slowly*). Right—and proper . . .

AUNT. As for the children, I spoke to the captain about *them!*

RONNIE. Did you?

AUNT. Staring at us every time we walk the deck! I told the captain exactly how we felt about the matter!

RONNIE. We?

AUNT. The things we talked about this morning!

RONNIE. Oh, yes, I remember. . . .

AUNT. I should think you would! You were quite definite in your opinion—and of course I agreed with you! They've no right to take such young children and bring them to New York to heaven knows what! (*Chuckles*) But you know the captain! That little charming smile, and he changed the subject and—oh, what difference does it make? We'll be docking in the morning, and away from all of it!

RONNIE. Aunt Mary, there's something I want to tell you that . . .

AUNT. No, no, tell me later, my dear! Right now the thing for you to do is to go down, get dressed, and join the others just as quickly as you can! (*Fade*) Come, now!

RONNIE. No. I want to stay here. . . .

AUNT (*back in*). Ronnie!

RONNIE. Please—a few moments longer. I'll come down. . . .

AUNT. Ronnie, I've never known you to— (*Gives up*) Oh, very well, have your silly little mood! I don't understand what it's about—mooning up here in the dark, like a romantic sixteen-year-old! All I say is, hurry downstairs. (*Fade*) We'll be waiting for you. . . .

(*Sound: Sigh of wind.*)

(*Music: Indicating stream of consciousness, behind.*)

RONNIE (*stream of consciousness*). Romantic—yes, it is romantic. . . . I'm in love with . . . (*Sighs*) If she knew—in love with . . .

(*Sound: We hear sigh of wind and patriotic strains far, far back as if heard on wind, fading quickly.*)

RONNIE (*laughs softly*). Yes. Love at twenty-third sight—with . . .

VOICE (*in close, whispers*). America . . .

RONNIE (*slowly*). That's a childish thought to have. . . .

VOICE (*whispers*). Patriotic pap. . . .

RONNIE (*stream of consciousness*). Of course it is—of course . . . Getting softening of the brain—thinking silly things—overemotionalized—ought to go below and join the party—stop standing here thinking to myself . . .

VOICE (*whispers*). America. . . .

RONNIE. No. Why shouldn't I think it out? How did it start?

AUNT (*whispering*). The things we talked about this morning. . . .

RONNIE. Yes, Aunt Mary *did* say that . . . "The things we talked about this morning."

VOICES. Those children!
    Always staring at us!
    Why bring them over?
    Full of foreign ideas!

7

Always staring!

(*Fade*)

Not like us!

Foreigners!

Not like us!

RONNIE (*quickly*). Not like us! I said that—I remember—not like us! Not like us—not like *me*! (*Slowly*) *Not like me.* . . . Resented their being on board! What happened? Let me remember . . . I went walking on the lower deck. They were sitting there as usual. . . .

VOICE (*whispers*). The four of them . . .

RONNIE. Yes, the four of them—sitting in a row—white faces staring, eyes looking at me—at me—at me. . . . I couldn't stand it. What did I say—yes, I said: (*Music: Out*) (*Up*) You! Children! Don't you know it's bad manners to stare at people? (*Music: Stream of consciousness, behind*) Faces lifted to me—didn't answer. I said: (*Music: Out*) (*Up*) Well! Didn't you hear me? One of you—answer me! You certainly understand *some* English, don't you? (*Music: Stream of consciousness, behind*) For a moment, no answer. Three little boys—one little girl. Their staring eyes . . . Why should they stare at me? I said: (*Music: Out*) (*Up*) Answer me, one of you! If you're coming to America —heaven knows why—at least they should have taught you some *English!* (*Music: Behind*) They didn't move. Four rigid little figures—and then: (*Music: Out.*)

JON (*off slightly*). We all speak English. . . .

RONNIE. Well! At last! The Sphinx speaks!

JON. No, that is not my name.

(*Music: Behind.*)

RONNIE. He said that, then he closed his mouth and the four of them were sitting there once again—those eyes of theirs

8

staring, staring. I said: (*Music: Out*) What are you sitting there for? I've been watching you all through the trip! You sit in those deck chairs hour after hour! Why don't you run around the deck—play! Answer me! Why don't you? What are you waiting for?

MIRIAM (*after pause, simply*). America. . . .

(*Music: Stream of consciousness, behind.*)

RONNIE. She said that, the little one, and then she closed her mouth so tightly I could see the muscles of the corners of her lips. She sat there—tense—frightened. Not another sound from any of them. Their eyes on me, through me— on the sea—the horizon! I said: (*Music: Out*) Land! All right, you're waiting for us to reach land, but what's that got to do with the four of you getting up, running around, having fun—yes, laughing! Why don't you laugh? What manner of kids are you? Don't you know how to laugh? *You*—do you know how?

JON. Yes.

RONNIE. And you?

SIEGFRIED. Yes.

RONNIE. How about you?

MIRIAM. Uh, huh.

RONNIE. And *you* know how to laugh?

ROBERT. Ja—(*Quickly*) yes.

RONNIE. Then laugh! Throw your heads back and laugh! The sun's shining, everyone's having fun! Laugh! Why don't you laugh?

(*Sound: Wind sighs.*)

ROBERT (*slowly*). When we are in America, we will laugh. . . .

RONNIE. So that's it! You don't like the sea! You're waiting for the land.

SIEGFRIED (*determinedly*). No. We are waiting for America. . . .

(*Music: Stream of consciousness, behind.*)

RONNIE. Waiting for America! What silly nonsense were these children thinking? Couldn't laugh until America! I thought to myself, how silly! Proves these children strangers, alien, foreign to our thought! Aloud I said: (*Music: Out*) Listen, the four of you—are you trying to rib me in your infant, continental manner? If you're waiting until you land, before you laugh, I'm warning you, you'd better start laughing now. There isn't much to laugh about there, let me assure you! The dullest, dumbest place on earth! Why do you think I went abroad? (*Scornfully*) Laugh in America! Don't make *me* laugh! We've got depressions and recessions and concessions and (*Fade*) dissensions and probes and investigations and this and that . . . (*Ad lib, fade far, far back.*)

(*Music: Stream of consciousness, behind.*)

RONNIE. And while I kept talking, the children's faces grew angrier and angrier—their eyes larger and larger—hating me for what I was saying—angrier and angrier until at last one of them cried:

(*Music and voices: Out—background ad lib out clean with:*)

ROBERT. No, no, wait!

RONNIE. Wait?

ROBERT. Miss American, wait! what you say—it is not right!

RONNIE. What's not right?

ROBERT. All these things you say of America, I do not understand. I do not know. But this I know—it is not right!

(*Other children join in "No! It is not right!" etc.*)

RONNIE (*amused*). Now, wait a moment, wait a moment! And what is right, *Herr* professors?

ROBERT. America is—is good, and a good place because—because— Jon, *you* say it!

JON. Because—because in America (*Hesitantly, as if groping to remember*) all men are—are . . .

SIEGFRIED. Created equal . . .

JON. Yes. And—and they are endow—endowed by—by . . .

MIRIAM. Their Creator with . . .

JON. With the right of Life—and—and . . .

ROBERT. Liberty . . .

JON. And liberty—and—and (*Quickly, triumphantly*) the 'suit of Happiness!

RONNIE. Bravo! Right out of the old Declaration of Independence! So where did you learn that and what does it mean?

MIRIAM. Jon teach us!

JON. *Ja* . . .

ROBERT (*correcting*). *Yes!*

JON (*amending quickly*). *Yes.* Here on the boat they gave me a book. I read—I—how you say it, Miss American?—I *teach!*

RONNIE (*down*). I see. And what you—uh—teach—all that about life and liberty and what have you—what can it possibly mean to four infants like you?

JON. Maybe I—I do not understand everything you say, Miss American, but what we learn, it means that no matter what is wrong in America, it can be fixed, because when we grow up we are free and equal and we can work and help America.

(*Music: Stream of consciousness.*)

RONNIE. Help America. . . . When he said that, I didn't have anything more to say—nothing cute or bright or clever. . . . Four little children. . . . I stood in front of them. Suddenly I wanted to say so many things to them, but my throat . . . I couldn't, I couldn't, until one of them said:

(*Music: Out*)

Siegfried (*almost tearfully*). Please, Miss American—what the books say about America—it is all right?

(*Sound: Hoot of ship's whistle, far back.*)

Ronnie (*fighting back her emotion*). Right. . . .

Jon. Tell us of it, Miss American.

Siegfried. *Bitte.*

Robert. Please.

Ronnie. It's—it's very large and very beautiful, and all the people in it or their fathers or their father's fathers came over the water to it just the way you're doing. And there's a bigness to it, and a braveness to it, and you need never be afraid, and no matter what goes wrong there, there's always hope as long as there's someone like you to remind the rest of us that the American way is—is the human way. . . .

(*Music: Stream of consciousness.*)

Ronnie. That's what I said to them—yes—and they came close to me and touched my hands and they smiled at each other and at me. . . . (*Sighs*) And so I'm in love—all over again—with my country—for remembering four little people —who want to help us.

(*Musical curtain.*)

SPECIAL TO HOLLYWOOD

I went to a Hollywood party. I didn't own a dress suit, and Eleanor's only evening gown was intended to hold back Lake Michigan's wind, not the sultry summer air of Beverly Hills. So we went as is—Eleanor in a peasant dress and her youth —and I in a tired burlap sack.

We had heard a great deal about the glamour of Hollywood gatherings, but we didn't go in any party excitement, because a few days before the gangsters had taken over Holland; it was hard to bubble with anticipation over anything, not even hors d'oeuvres catered by Ciro's.

We climbed the usual hill to the usual "My-God-what-kind-of-architecture-is-this" style of Hollywood mansion, and our first Hollywood dinner party began.

It was just as we had anticipated: a beautifully set table and a beautiful service and enough uncovered bosoms to mother the world.

Eleanor and I had wondered what these motion-picture master-minds would discuss. But the courses came and went, and the conversation carefully skirted anything with any more meaning than who was where with whom and why. I thought to myself, "Thoughtful of them. Good taste. Blitzkriegs do things to the glands of digestive secretion."

Dinner over, we all went into a Grand-Central-station sitting room. Now it would begin, I thought. These top producers and directors and writers and actors and actresses would pin Mr. Shickelgruber and his gang to the wall. They did. But not quite as I had anticipated.

14

Mr. Director. *I'm telling you, people aren't going to want anything with ideas. Escape, that's it. Screwball comedies. I tell you, the only way we're going to beat this war is to give people things to laugh at.*

Mr. Producer. *Gonna have to cut budgets all the way around, yes, sir! Those damned unions will have to fall in line or we'll all go out of business, and then where will they be?*

Mr. Actor. *If they think they're going to use this war to cut down on my salary they've got another think coming!*

Mr. Writer. *So I said to my agent, "Arthur," I said, "Arthur, if you let them feed you that baloney about losing foreign markets and having to cut salaries, I'm switching to the Hayward office and you can take your contract and put it up your Duesenburg!"*

Here we go again! I began to boil. Again this terrific immorality, this basic disregard of what was vital, this blindness to the wave of disaster that was sweeping toward us.

When Joe Doaks boils, he finds release by going to a ball game or beating his wife; there wasn't a ball game in sight, and my wife knew jujitsu, so I wrote Special to Hollywood.

(*Sound of airplane moving along in the sky, down slightly, and continuing behind.*)

MARK. Now, look here, pilot, can't you make this thing go faster?

SAM (*mildly*). Sorry. What did you say?

MARK. Take those infernal ear-phones or whatever they are off your head and listen to me! I said can't you make this thing go faster?

SAM. A hundred and fifty miles an hour isn't exactly walking, mister!

MARK. Now, don't get impertinent! I chartered this special plane for speed, you understand—speed—not to just go dawdling along through the air!

SAM. I'll tell him about it when he comes in.

MARK. Now—now look here! Do you realize who you're talking to?

SAM. Look here, mister—I'll be the first to admit you're a big shot—but when you're bucking a fifty-mile wind and still making a hundred and fifty miles an hour, believe me, that's pretty good! Now, why don't you go back in the cabin and sit down and enjoy yourself, like a good fella?

MARK (*spluttering*). Now—now look here! You can't tell me what to do! You can't . . .

LONA (*back, muffled as if she were back in the cabin*). Mark! Mark! Come here! Mark, I'm talking to you!

MARK (*every time she talks to him he crawls*). Coming, darling! (*Fade*) Coming!

(*Door of plane opening, back.*)

LONA (*far back*). For Pete's sake, Mark, where you been? Do I have to split a lung every time I want to talk to you?

MARK (*back*). All right, darling, all right! I'm here!

(*Closing cabin door, back. From this point on all voices in the cabin become muffled and are barely distinguishable.*)

LONA (*back, far back, muffled*). Did you tell him to hurry up?

MARK (*muffled, far back*). Yes, yes. Everything taken care of!

LONA. That's what *you* say! I'm sick of this! I want to get home!

MARK. Be there in two hours!

LONA. That's what you say! You said we had plenty of Scotch, too!

MARK. Well, I thought . . .

LONA. Oh, you make me tired! I don't know why I went on this trip, anyway!

MARK (*fade back*). Good publicity.

LONA (*back*). Publicity! Publicity! I can sit in my back yard and get publicity!

MARK. Oh, Lona, darling!

LONA. Don't Lona darling me. Where can I get a drink? What are you good for, anyway?

MARK. Now, look here. If not for me, where would you be?

LONA. *You* tell *me!*

MARK. Everybody in Hollywood knows!

LONA. Everybody? Who's everybody?

SAM (*talking into his communications microphone*). NC 19 calling Glendale . . . NC 19 calling Glendale. . . . Hello, Joe. How is it? Yeah? Well, the farmers like it. Huh? Oh, yeah, everything's "normal" here. Listen!

(*For a few seconds all we hear are muffled, high-pitched voices from cabin.*)

SAM. Yeah! No, that's only two of 'em. When the third guy starts in—boy! Okay, tell them to get the studio brass band ready. We'll be settin' down in a couple hours. Okay. . . . NC 19 signing off.

(*Sound of airplane and the muffled, unintelligible conversation back in the cabin for a few seconds then, on cue, the conversation in the cabin becomes intelligible.*)

LONA (*fade-in, muffled for a few seconds, then clearly*). You heard what I said! How many times do I have to say it? You heard me the first time! If not for me being in it, that picture would stink so loud the only way anyone could go see it would be with one of those gas things on their face!

MARK. But, darling, be reasonable! Any picture that nets three hundred thousand dollars the first week . . .

LONA. Because I'm in it, that's why! Because I'm in it! Isn't that right, Bob?

BOB. Huh? What did you say?

LONA. Oh, for Pete's sake, take your nose out of that racing form and listen to me, will you?

BOB. Listen yourself, beautiful—I'm busy.

LONA (*furiously*). Mark, you tell me—how long do I have to put up with this lily imitation of a louse?

MARK. Now, Lona, darling . . .

BOB. It's all right, Mark, it's all right! I can take it—for a thousand a week!

LONA. Mark, are you going to let him talk to me like that?

MARK. He—he hasn't said anything!

BOB. She's reading my mind!

LONA. Why, you two-bit little fourflusher, let me tell you . . .

BOB. What do you mean, fourflusher? Why, if not for me

shoving your name in every newspaper in the country, you'd be back in the laundry!

LONA. Mark! Mark, did you hear that?

MARK. Now, Bob, watch yourself! After all . . .

BOB. You keep out of this!

LONA. Fire him! Fire him! (*Continue.*)

BOB. Yeah, sure, fire me! Go on! So I'll go to work for Warner's tomorrow! (*"Fire him!"*) Yeah, fire me! Then I'll have some decent pictures to go to town on instead (*"Throw him out!"*) of this baby's turkeys!

LONA. Turkeys!

MARK. Now, Bob, don't go too far! After all . . .

LONA. Did you hear him? My pictures turkeys! Three hundred thousand dollars the first week . . .

BOB. Why? Ask me why? Exploitation, that's it. Uh, why, without my publicity, you wouldn't be *back* in the laundry, you'd be *in* it!

LONA (*completely losing temper*). Why, you—you little squirt, you! I'll—I'll scratch your eyes out!

BOB. You lay a hand on me, I'll slap you down!

LONA. Mark! Mark, *do* something.

MARK. You're fired! You hear me, Bob? Fired!

BOB. Why, you big bag of wind, who do you think you're firing?

LONA. Mark, throw him out.

BOB. Why, I'll go to J.B. and I'll have him cut your heart out!

MARK. Fired, I tell you!

LONA. Out on your ear!

BOB. You're not a producer—you're a fugitive from the laundry *she* used to work in!

Lona. Blacklist him, Mark! Have him blacklisted! (*Continue.*)

Bob. Metro, Zanuck, Wanger—why, I can walk into a dozen jobs tomorrow morning!

Mark. I'll run you out of Hollywood!

Lona. You'll—you'll starve to death, and I'll kick you in the face! You won't get another job in Hollywood if I have to . . . (*Breaks out, and cries out in fright as airplane zooms up suddenly.*)

Mark. That crazy pilot!

Bob. What's he doing?

Lona. Tell him to stop!

(*Airplane straightened out, motor roar down and continuing back behind.*)

Mark. Crazy fool! Climbing like that!

Lona. Don't stand there! Go on—give him the devil!

Mark. All right, I'm going. (*Fade*) All right!

(*Cabin door open, back.*)

Mark (*back*). Hey, you! Pilot! You crazy!

Sam (*back*). It's all right, mister. Had to climb! Storm ahead!

Mark. Who cares about the storm? You get us home, understand?

Sam (*back*). Okay, you're payin' for it! Here—message for you came over the radio.

Mark (*back*). All right, all right, hand it over!

Lona (*up*). What is it, Mark? For me?

(*Cabin door closing, far back.*)

Mark (*fade-in*). No—me. Yeah, me. . . .

Bob. What's up? Huh?

Lona. Mark, what's the matter with you? Mouth open like a fish! Read it!

MARK (*obviously very disturbed*). It's—it—it says that John
 Webster killed himself.

BOB. Say!

LONA. You're—you're kidding!

MARK. See for yourself!

(*Rattle of paper.*)

LONA (*reads quickly*). John Webster, young novelist, committed suicide 1 P.M.

BOB. I never thought—he'd do it. . . .

MARK. I—didn't either. . . . Killing himself—just because **we**
 changed . . .

BOB. Yeah. . . .

(LONA *laughs softly.*)

BOB. You—laughing?

LONA. Sure, why not?

MARK. Now, Lona, darling, after all . . .

LONA (*harshly*). After all, *what?* Two wise guys, and neither
 one of you's got as many brains as the—the left side of **my**
 Pekingese!

BOB. Okay, let's have it!

LONA. You—the great Mr. Crane—the publicity wonder-boy!

BOB. Cut out the needles, will you, and let's have it!

MARK. Yes, Lona! What are you getting at?

LONA. So he's dead, so instead of looking down your noses,
 you two ought to be standing on your heads!

MARK. Wha' . . .

BOB. She's nuts!

LONA. Oh, am I? The picture getting national release this
 week, and the sap who writes the words blows his brains
 out, and I'm supposed to cry, eh?

BOB. Say! I get it!

LONA. Call out the Marines!

MARK. Lona, you—you mean that now he can't bother us with an injunction?

LONA. Who's thinking about injunctions? He couldn't stop the picture anyway. You said yourself he signed away all the rights!

MARK. Then what . . .

LONA. Oh, you tell him, Bob!

BOB. It's terrific! Mark, don't you get it?

MARK. Huh?

BOB. So we had the première in Chicago—so all right, it stunk!

LONA. Don't you start in that again, or I'll . . .

BOB. Okay, okay, it wasn't your fault. The director was no good. The film was no good. The cutters got the story loused up. The critics all had bellyaches. What's the difference what the reason was? The picture was a floperoo—laid eggs all the way up and down State Street!

MARK. Get to the point!

BOB. I've passed it already! Don't you get it? The author of the novel we made the film out of blows his top! Why? Ask me? Why?

MARK. I don't have to ask you! The kid told me yesterday right in the hotel! Ruined his life-work, he said!

BOB. Yeah, that's what *he* said. But it won't be what *I'll* say!

MARK. Huh? Wha' . . . Who?

LONA. Oh, for Pete's sake, Mark, shut your mouth, and listen to the guy! For the first time in a year he's got a good idea —*my* idea!

BOB. That's what *you* think! Listen, Mark, with this angle we can turn the picture into a gold mine!

MARK. Well, say it, say it!

Lona. *I'll* say it! The reason that crazy kid killed himself was because the picture was so terrific, he was done, finished!

Bob. Yeah, yeah, his life-work comes to life on the silver screen, so the boy genius bows out! Don't you get it?

Mark. But—but that isn't true!

Lona. Oh, for the lova . . .

Mark. I mean, who'll believe you? It's—it's crazy!

Bob. Will you listen to the guy, Lona? Crazy!

Mark. Sure, crazy! A story like that—no newspaper'll believe it!

Bob. Oh, won't they? How about if you have a letter the kid wrote you just before he—you know—did it!

Lona. That's all right!

Mark. But he didn't write me any such letter!

Bob. Oh, for— Lona, *you* tell him!

Lona. Mark, what're you trying to do—give an imitation of Dopey? Did the sappy kid have to write a letter? Aren't there plenty of guys you got at the studio who'll write you a letter like that for ten bucks?

Bob. Yeah, and give you change of five?

Lona. Aren't there?

Mark. Oh!

Bob. *Oh* is right! Why, the kid's bumping himself off is a natural!

Lona. And who thought of it first? *You* tell *me!*

(*Loud burst of thunder. Everyone cries out in fright.*)

Mark. Storm!

Bob. What kind of a screwy pilot we got?

(*Thunder again.*)

Lona. Mark, don't stand there! *Do* something!

Mark. All right, all right! (*Fade*) I'll talk to him!

(*Thunder again.*)

LONA. Bob! So dark! The lights!

BOB. Can't find the switch! Ah—there!

(*Thunder again.*)

LONA (*up*). Mark! Mark, tell him to get us out of this!

BOB. Gee, is it dark out there!

LONA. You two fat-heads—I told you I didn't want to go to Chicago! (*Up*) Mark! Mark, tell him to get us out of the storm! Mark, you hear me! (*Up*) Mark!

(*Thunder again.*)

BOB. I'll go see . . .

LONA. No! Don't leave me!

BOB. Okay, okay!

(*Airplane begins climbing.*)

BOB. Listen! We're climbing!

LONA. Climbing? So what does that mean?

BOB. He's taking us above the storm!

(*Thunder back a little.*)

LONA. Well, why doesn't he hurry? I hate thunder! (*Up*) Mark!

(*Thunder back farther.*)

MARK (*fade-in*). It's all right, darling, it's all right!

LONA. What's all right! *What!*

MARK. He's getting us up over the top of the storm!

BOB. Yeah, like I told you!

LONA. What did the buzzard get us into this for in the first place? If you don't get him fired I'll . . .

(*Thunder far, far back.*)

MARK. There we are! In the light again!

BOB. Will you look at those clouds down there!

LONA. So who cares! Oh, what I'd give for a Scotch!

MARK. We'll be home soon!

BOB. You can't even see the ground! Like a carpet from there!

LONA. Oh, will you shut up! Who cares about clouds?

BOB. Listen, toots-en-frootz, who's talking to you?

LONA. Mark! Did you hear what he said to me?

MARK. Now, now, don't start again, the two of you! I've had all I can stand these three days!

LONA. *You've* had! Will you listen to the guy! Who was pulled and pushed around by everyone from the Cicero Fan Club No. One to those flop-eared exhibitors to those louse reporters to . . .

BOB. Hey, wait a minute!

LONA. Huh?

MARK. Whassamatter?

BOB. I got an idea! Listen! That screwy author . . . When we land I'll have a wire sent . . . We'll have the body sent to the coast and bury him at the studio's expense!

MARK. Huh?

BOB. Yeah, sort of a state funeral for the author of the Lona Douglas' greatest vehicle!

LONA. That's all right!

MARK. I dunno. Maybe they won't . . .

BOB. *Who* won't? The kid didn't have anybody—so we'll do the honors, see? Special car all across the country . . . Make every news service in the world!

MARK. I don't know. I don't know. Morbid—you know—morbid—I dunno . . .

LONA. That's the trouble, you don't know! The first good idea this lily's had since . . .

BOB. Now, wait a minute . . .

LONA. And you start getting artistic or something! Well, let me tell you . . . Hey, what's the matter with you? Mark! I'm talking to you!

MARK. Listen!

LONA. Huh?

BOB. What the . . .

MARK. Bob! You . . .

LONA. What's the matter with you two?

BOB. Engines . . .

LONA. Huh?

MARK. The engine! It's stopped!

LONA. So what? We're landing! What's the matter with you two saps? Shut off the engine because we're landing!

MARK. N-no . . .

BOB (*up*). Pilot! (*Fade*) Pilot! Pilot, what's the matter? (*Far back*) Pilot, what's happened?

SAM (*far back*). I don't know. I don't!

BOB. What is it? What's happened?

(BOB *and pilot continue ad lib far, far back, discussing engine failure.*)

LONA (*on cue through above*). What *is* this? Mark, what did he chase off for? What's the matter? We *are* landing, aren't we? Then what's there to get so excited about?

MARK. The—the engine stopped.

LONA. Will you stop saying that? So *what?*

MARK. W-we're not due in for an hour yet!

LONA. Something's wrong! (*Fading*) Pilot! Pilot, what's the matter? Pilot!

MARK (*through above fade*). Lona! Lona, wait! Lona!

(*Fast fade-in of* BOB *and* LONA *talking away a mile a minute to pilot. Ad libs, such as "What's the big idea?"—"Why are we landing here?"—"What's the matter with the engine?" —"What kind of a pilot are you, anyway?" etc.*)

MARK (*joins in*). No, no, let me talk to him! Listen, you, what's the matter? Why don't you answer? I'm paying for this, answer *me!* What are you up to?

SAM (*on cue*). Shut up! Shut up, all of you! *Shut up, I say!*
(*The others stop.*)

SAM (*tensely*). We're not landing, see? *We're not landing!*

MARK. But—but the engines!

BOB. They're stopped! We *must* be landing!
(*All three—LONA, MARK and BOB begin again.*)

SAM. Shut up! Blast you, shut up!

MARK. You can't talk to her that way!

LONA. Sock him!

BOB. Who do you think you're talking to?

SAM. You fools, will you shut up? Look! Look, I tell you!

MARK (*after pause, nervously*). At—at what?

SAM. The indicator! Air-speed indicator!

BOB. Huh?

SAM. *We're not falling!*

LONA. Mark, what's he saying?

SAM. Listen! I'm *telling* you! We're not falling! Engine's dead —and we're not falling! You fools! What are you looking at me like that for? Don't you understand? We're hanging —just hanging in the air!
(*Musical transition.*)

MARK (*softly, dazedly*). Hanging . . . Air . . .

LONA (*begins softly, slowly, tensely*). You dirty-faced buzzard, what're you trying to pull? (*Up. Almost shriekingly*) What're you trying to pull?

SAM. Prop dead. Just hanging in air . . .

MARK. Hanging . . . Air . . .

LONA (*down again, tensely*). Listen, the three of you. I've been around—they've pulled all kinds of fancy tricks on me— (*Building*) Well, if this is a gag, I don't like it! You hear me? I don't like it! Get me down out of here!

(BOB *sighs. Thud of body back as he faints.*)

LONA. Bob! (*Dazedly*) He—he's passed out!

SAM (*down*). Come on—back in the cabin—better sit down. Mr. Markam, you too. . . .

LONA. Bob . . . He . . .

SAM. He'll be all right. Come on. . . .

MARK (*dazedly*). Hanging—in air . . .

LONA. This—this is a gag, isn't it? Tell me! Isn't it? We're moving! We've got to be moving! Talk, blast you! Talk!

SAM. Lady, my arm—cut it out, will ya!

LONA. Then tell me! What's happening? What? Bob passed out. Mark lookin' like—his mouth—he . . . You've *got* to talk! You've got to tell me! We are moving, aren't we?

SAM. No. . . .

LONA. You liar! You dirty liar! We *are!* We *are!*

SAM. Stop it! Look! Down there!

LONA. You dirty liar! Trying to scare me!

SAM. Look! See—on the clouds down there! Huh—our shadow—standing still! We're not moving! Get it through your head! We're hanging in space, I tell you!

(LONA *begins to moan. Moan builds until she bursts into tears of semi-hysteria.*)

(*Musical transition.*)

BOB (*weakly*). I—I'm all right. Just—just leave me alone. . . .

SAM. Hit your head, when you . . .

BOB (*sharply*). Leave me alone, I tell you! What're you all sitting around looking at me for? I—I passed out—all right. You're all just as scared as I am! You know it! You are! You, Mark, you *are* scared. Your face green . . . Answer me—you are scared, aren't you?

28

MARK (*dazedly, slowly*). Hanging—in air . . .

BOB. There, you see—off his nut! You—Lona—you're scared, too, aren't you?

LONA. Why—don't—you—shut up . . . ?

BOB. Pilot! You! You're scared green, too, aren't you? Not me alone—*you!* Answer me! *You!*

SAM (*quietly, grimly*). Maybe I'd better shut you up. . . .

BOB (*pitifully, tears in voice*). I'm scared. . . . I'm scared. . . . I'm scared. . . . (*Cries.*)

LONA (*harshly soothing*). All right, Bob, all right. . . .

BOB. Lona, I don't want to . . .

LONA. All right, now, all right. Don't talk. . . . Bury your head. . . . Yeah, that's right. . . .

(BOB *continues to cry softly behind the following.*)

LONA. Pilot! Oh, Sam . . .

SAM. Yeah?

LONA. What time is it?

SAM. Five. . . .

LONA. The radio. . . .

SAM. What's the use? Tried it a hundred times. . . . Dead as—as . . .

LONA. We're goin' to be . . . ?

(BOB *moans anew.*)

LONA. Don't listen to what we're talking about, Bob. Just try—not to think. . . . Sam. . . .

SAM. Yeah?

LONA. How long have we been . . . ?

SAM. An hour. . . .

LONA. Only that?

SAM. Seems like a million . . . But—watch says only an hour. . . .

LONA. Mark! Mark, listen . . . Mark, I'm talking to you!

MARK (*back—dazedly as before*). Hanging—air . . .

LONA. I—I wish I was like he is. . . .

SAM. Yeah. . . .

LONA. So scared can't see or hear—or think—look . . .

SAM. Huh?

LONA. He's gone to sleep. Bob . . .

SAM. Yeah. . . .

LONA. Wore himself out crying . . . Funny, huh?

SAM. Nothing's funny. . . .

LONA. Guess not. . . . But I got funny thoughts in my head . . .

SAM. What?

LONA. A minute ago I was thinking about when I was a kid. . . . Want to hear about when I was a kid?

SAM. Why not?

LONA. Bob, here, and all the rest of the publicity guys have wrote—written—so much junk about me being the only daughter of—you know—poor but respectable small-town people that I almost got to thinking it was true. Yeah—would you believe it? I paid some wise guy over on Sunset Boulevard a thousand bucks for a coat-of-arms of the family to hang up in the hall. You know, one of those fancy shields with lions crawling all over it, and things. . . . Should have had a couple of beer bottles on it instead of lions . . . Yeah. . . . You want to know my real name? Aw, what's the difference? Beer bottles—yeah—beer bottles and the smell of the laundry coming up the air-shaft and a lot of dirt—that's what I remember from when I was a kid . . . (*Pause*) Sam. . . .

SAM. Yeah?

LONA. I just wanted to hear you talk. What was I talking about? Oh, yeah, I was thinking of something funny about when I was a kid. When it was hot at night I used to lie on my back on the roof and look at the clouds and make out I was just sort of hanging in the air. . . . Honest, Sam, I'd want that. . . . Funny now, huh . . . ?

SAM. Gravity. . . .

LONA. What?

SAM. Did I say something?

LONA. You said "gravity." Why?

SAM. I was thinking. . . .

LONA. What?

SAM. Gravity's pulling us down.

LONA. Well?

SAM. I was thinking of what's pulling us up. . . .

LONA. There aren't any answers. . . .

SAM. No?

LONA. No—no answers. When I was that kid I found answers. Yeah, how to get along—how to get out of that smell and that dirt—real answers. . . . They took me a long way. . . . Five thousand a week—five-year contract—no options —I did all right with my answers! But here's one answer I haven't got—because there *isn't* any answer!

SAM. Maybe there is. . . .

LONA. Yeah?

SAM. Yeah. . . .

LONA. You listened to me—supposing *I* listen to *you*. . . .

SAM. I don't know how to talk. . . .

LONA. Just—go ahead . . .

SAM. For a whole hour I've been tryin' to figure things out. . . .

LONA. So . . .

SAM. There isn't any real answer. . . . I mean that adds up like a column of figures on a slide rule when you're—you're

tryin' to figure out the stress on a wing—nothing like that
. . . But a kinda screwy idea's come to me . . . Ah, why
talk about it!

LONA. Go on!

SAM. I'm just a bozo. Ever since I've been able to stand on
my own feet everything's got to be able to add up, or it
just doesn't mean anything to me. . . . But when I was a
kid . . .

LONA. Well?

SAM. Well, when I was a kid I really had the—well, like you
said—poor but respectable parents. You know the kind . . .
They believed in somebody up there and somebody down
below and good and evil and all the rest of it! Funny, you
thinkin' about when you were a kid . . . And me thinkin'
the same thing . . .

LONA. You said you had the answers. . . .

SAM (*he starts slowly, building in intensity*). Yeah. It's like
this: I heard the three of you talkin' all the way from the
Coast to Chicago and now back again. Talkin' about nothing but yourselves—each one of you—nothin' meanin' anything but yourselves . . . If we weren't like this up here, I
know I wouldn't be able to say this, but—well, why not say
it? You—you makin' more money in a week than the average guy with a family sweats out his insides for in a year.
But, instead of the money makin' you understand anything,
it's made you understand less than a blind kid walkin' in
the dark! Everything's for you; the world's just a big movie
screen and everybody's in it just there to sit up and look
at you! Everything's for you; even when they're dead they're
for you! Yeah, I heard. Somebody wrote a book and you
bought it and made a picture out of it, and maybe it was
an honest book, but you didn't buy it to be honest, you

bought it to make dough; so the kid blew his brains out, and even dead he couldn't get away from you! Yeah, you were goin' to use his dead body to make you more money! Yeah, dead or alive, nothin' means anything to you! There's no world but your screwy world. Everybody all over the world can crawl in the ground hidin' from bombs, can be starved and watch their kids starve, and die on barbed wire fightin' for something they don't know much about and drown in the sea, and it don't mean anything to you—none of it—as long as each of you can hold on to what you've got! Yeah, the three of you actin' as if you weren't made of the same flesh and blood as the rest of us—as if makin' a lot of money and seein' your name in the paper a lot and gettin' a lot of applause, took you right off the earth! (*Slowly*) Well, maybe something or somebody decided you weren't fit for the earth. . . . maybe . . .

LONA. Maybe . . .

SAM. You—you cryin'?

LONA (*tears in her voice*). No.

SAM. You asked me—I told you. . . .

LONA (*slowly*). I was in a picture once. . . . The girl got in a jam . . . She didn't know how to pray, but she started to pray. . . . That was in a picture—and this is real, isn't it?

SAM. Yeah. . . .

LONA. If anybody told me a couple of hours ago that all this— Mark, sitting there, out of his head—Bob—me sitting here listening to the kind of thing you said . . .

SAM. You asked me—I told you. . . .

LONA. Yeah. You told me. . . . It *was* a lousy trick, wasn't it?

SAM. Huh?

LONA. About that kid who died . . . I'm sorry about that. . . . Even thinking about it . . . I'm sorry. . . .

(*As she says the words the airplane motor suddenly starts up again. They both cry out in surprise.*)

SAM. The engine!

LONA. We've started again!

(*Plane goes into a dive.*)

SAM. We're in a dive! (*Fade*) Got to get it!

LONA. Mark! Bob! We're moving again! Mark! Bob!

(*Plane comes out of dive and levels off.*)

SAM (*back, calling*). It's all right! Everything's all right!

LONA. Mark! Bob! Wake up! Snap out of it! Do you hear? Everything's all right!

(*Musical transition.*)

(*Board fade-in of airplane moving along at normal speed together with:*)

MARK. All right! All right! So it's settled! All right!

BOB. Sure, it's settled! I know my publicity—a thing like this isn't good—it's bad!

MARK. I'm not arguing with you! All right!

BOB. Spread a screwy thing like this, and every reporter in the country would hold his nose! It's too screwy, that's all!

MARK. For Heaven's sake, will you stop talkin' about it! For the last hour . . . My head's starting to go around! It's forgotten—finished—so whatever it was, we'll forget it!

BOB. Wait! The pilot! Did you talk to him?

MARK. Sure, sure, he won't talk! He wants to eat, don't he? So he won't talk!

LONA (*slowly*). You've got everything fixed, eh?

BOB. Well! The prima donna's talkin' again!

MARK. Now, Lona, you understand, nobody's going to know about this! Like Bob says—crazy publicity is bad publicity and—and this all *was* crazy, wasn't it?

BOB. I'll say! Look! We're over the airport!

MARK. Good! Good! Drink—do I need a drink!

BOB. A bathtub full! I'm going to swim in it!

MARK. A terrible experience—terrible! But all's well that ends well, eh, Lona? A terrible experience but now—finished! Everything's just the same! Eh, Lona? Everything's just the same!

LONA (*in close, slowly*). I wonder . . .

(*Up, with airplane sound slightly as transition, then down and continuing back behind.*)

SAM. NC 19 coming in—NC 19 coming in. Hello, Joe. . . . Yeah, had a little trouble—a while back—yeah—uh—engine trouble. Yeah, everything's back to normal now. Yeah, everybody okay. Everything just the same. (*In close, down*) I wonder . . .

(*Musical curtain.*)

SOLE SURVIVORS

Dear Just-Graduated-from-a-Journalism-Class:

I have a sure-fire three-word formula for your success, now that you've gone into business. It's a three-word formula that's guaranteed to give you security and social standing or your money back. It's a formula that has worked for years in many times and many climes; so, if you want to know how to win friends and never get in a concentration camp, listen closely. This is the open sesame to the full, fat life:

"Play It Safe!"

Oh, you don't think that's quite detailed enough. All right —let me write on the back of your diploma and I'll give you some addenda.

(a) Never take sides. Taking sides alienates people because some of them may not agree with you.

(b) Don't try any new technics. Pioneering is always profitless.

(c) Write the same story long enough and you will build up a "following."

Let us consider (a) in some detail. First, definitely don't discuss national affairs. Believe that this is the best of all possible economies, and if you mention the fact that some people have much too little and others much too much, be certain to point out that the have-nots haven't because (a) they will eventually, (b) they're radicals, (c) any man can get work if he really wants to.

Don't discuss international affairs because (a) you never know with whom you'll have to do business eventually, (b) it might antagonize them.

38

Consider the wisdom of this practice in the light of the end results. Never having written anything controversial, you will retain a full quantity of friends. The middle-of-the-fencers will understand you, the right-wingers will ignore you, and those at the left will find you amusingly beneath their consideration, and so will leave you safely and peacefully alone.

As to the foolishness of trying the new technics, that's self-apparent. People have become accustomed to a certain type of story, and that's what they want and you should give it to them. If you don't, you're taking a chance on their not understanding you or disagreeing with you, and so you split your market and your possible income.

So, dear little Just-Graduated-from-Journalism-School, play your typewriter close to your chest and the money pot will be yours.

SOLE SURVIVORS

ANNOUNCER. The scene: aboard the U. S. destroyer *Liberty* somewhere in the Mediterranean. It is dusk; the usual disciplined calm of the battleship has been broken, for the past half hour, by a minor tragedy of the sea. In the heavy fog a small fishing skiff has been cut down by the lunging prow of the destroyer. At the moment, the senior officer is making his report to the commandant.

LIEUTENANT (*fade-in*). . . . And there's no doubt, sir, from the testimony of the men on deck, that not only was the skiff operatin' without a foghorn, but she didn't have a light on her, neither, fore or aft.

COMMANDANT. That's all very well, lieutenant, but what I want to know is how about the boy?

LIEUTENANT. Oh, he's all right, sir. Not a thing wrong with him. Raisin' the devil good and proper, that he is, sir!

COMMANDANT. Eh? What do you mean?

LIEUTENANT. Well, sir, it's a boat he wants!

COMMANDANT (*sharply*). A boat?

LIEUTENANT. Aye, sir! The minute he hit the deck he began yellin' for a boat in place of the one we ran down, and, so help me, sir, he's been at it ever since—yellin' and cussin'— in every lingo from Spik to Malay Dutch!

COMMANDANT. Put him below deck until morning!

LIEUTENANT. But that won't help, sir! It's the baby got us worried!

COMMANDANT (*sharply*). Baby?

40

LIEUTENANT. Aye, sir. Baby, sir—the one the lad brought with him!

COMMANDANT (*ominously*). If this is your idea of a joke, lieutenant . . .

LIEUTENANT. Oh, no, sir! It's a baby, right enough! Ten or twelve months old is how I rate it.

COMMANDANT (*frigidly*). Lieutenant, perhaps you're not aware that I saw the boy brought over the side? He was *alone!*

LIEUTENANT. Aye, sir, but all the time he had this kid, I mean this baby, wrapped up snug under his coat. Didn't know it was there, we didn't, until all at once he takes it out and starts dressin' it in the dry stuff we gave him.

COMMANDANT. Well, I'll be . . . !

LIEUTENANT. Aye, sir.

COMMANDANT. Whose baby is it? Who is the boy? What was he doing out here in the fog in a small boat without running lights?

LIEUTENANT. Well, that's just it, sir. He won't tell us!

COMMANDANT. Eh?

LIEUTENANT. Just keeps yellin' for a boat right away quick, *vité,* pronto, and all the rest of it! Got the kid under one arm, and wavin' his fist yellin' to see the captain! And the baby yellin' with him! It's one helluva mess, sir!

(*Sound of baby squalling and boy talking loudly but intelligibly far back, muffled as if through door.*)

LIEUTENANT. There, sir! Hear 'em?

COMMANDANT (*sharply*). Send him in.

LIEUTENANT (*fade*). Aye, sir.

(*Door opening back—up on baby's crying.*)

LIEUTENANT (*back*). You! Boy! The Commander'll see you! (*Impatiently*) In here! In here! (*In a little*) This is him, sir. I mean *them.*

COMMANDANT. Very good, lieutenant.

LIEUTENANT (*fade*). Aye, sir.

(*Door closing, back.*)

COMMANDANT. Come closer, boy. . . .

(*Fade-in baby crying.*)

COMMANDANT. Boy, can't you do something about that—that child?

JUAN (*he is about fourteen; the horrors he has lived through are in his voice*). You are the capitan, señor?

COMMANDANT. I'm Commander Roberts. Now, that baby—can't you do something about him?

JUAN (*with dignity*). Her, señor. . . .

COMMANDANT. Ah. . . .

JUAN (*softly, soothingly*). Quiet, little flower. . . . Yes, this is the capitan. . . . He will help us. Quiet, little sister. . . .

(*Baby stops crying behind above.*)

COMMANDANT. Well! He—*she* certainly listens to you!

JUAN. As you will listen to me, capitan! A boat—you will give me a boat!

(*Baby gurgles sleepily.*)

COMMANDANT. Look, boy, you're carrying quite an armful there—why not sit down?

JUAN. I have not time, señor! A boat! I must have a boat! Quickly! Do not stand there!

COMMANDANT (*sharply*). All right, boy, that's about enough of that! You'll be taken care of.

JUAN. You mean that, señor?

COMMANDANT. Certainly!

JUAN. Then you *will* give me a boat—*now?*

COMMANDANT. Boy, try and understand! This is a government ship. The facts of your case will be placed before the proper authorities. I am sure proper compensation will be made for your loss.

JUAN. The—the words, señor—all of them I do not understan'! This I know: a boat—give me a boat, señor! There is no time! We must go! We . . .

COMMANDANT (*interrupting sharply*). Stop that! Didn't you hear me? I said you'd be taken care of! You and your sister —we'll get you back where you belong. Is that clear?

JUAN (*after a pause, slowly*). A hole in the ground . . .

COMMANDANT. Eh?

JUAN (*slowly*). A hole in the ground is good enough for me, señor, but my sister . . . I do not think even you would want that for her. . . .

COMMANDANT. What are you talking about?

JUAN. You said you will take us back where we came from. . . .

COMMANDANT. Well?

JUAN. The bombs made—great holes, señor. . . .

(*We hear the blast of the ship's whistle, back.*)

COMMANDANT (*down*). Where are you from?

JUAN. Aguila. . . .

COMMANDANT. Ah. . . .

(*Baby gurgles sleepily.*)

JUAN (*pleading*). My sister asks you, too. . . . You will give us another boat, señor?

COMMANDANT. Your—family?

JUAN (*explosively*). I told you, señor! I told you! Hole in the ground!

COMMANDANT. I'm sorry. (*Sotto, almost to himself*) Aguila— that's two hundred miles from the sea. . . . Battle area . . . Boy, how did you manage to . . . ? You don't mind answering a few questions, do you?

JUAN. Questions? Questions, señor? *You* ask *me?* No! I have questions I have wanted to ask for many days. *You* have gray hair—*you* are old—they always tell me the old are *wise!* So now *you* tell *me*, señor!

COMMANDANT. Wha—

JUAN. Señor, *why did they die?*

COMMANDANT. Oh, well . . . It's war, boy. . . . A difference of ideas. . . . Some day you'll understand. . . .

JUAN. Understand, señor? What is there to understand? Pepé —he understood to milk the cow! Jiminez understood how to make the baskets to sell in the marketplace! Teresa—she understand how to beat the clothes white on the stones of the river! Juana, how to take care of her five children! But war, señor! It was so good in our village—the sun so bright —the air so clear—what had we to do with war? *Make* me understand, señor! *Why are they all dead?*

COMMANDANT (*uncomfortably*). Well—uh—a civil war . . . As I said, a difference of ideas . . . How can I explain . . . ?

JUAN. My papa tell to me many things. He talk to me of a world where men think free and talk free, where everybody has his own land, not too much, and men are like brothers. Is this why my papa is dead, señor? Is this why bombs drop from the sky?

COMMANDANT. Boy, listen to me . . . !

JUAN. No, señor, you do not know! You are not wise! No one who is old is wise! I must go! A boat, señor! Give me my boat!

COMMANDANT. But, boy . . .

(*Baby laughs.*)

JUAN. Listen to her, señor! Our village was full of such laughter! Where is it now? Only Maruja and me, but her I take

44

away to some place where there is nobody old and wise to drop bombs on her!

COMMANDANT. So *that's* where you were sailing!

JUAN. *Si! Si!* We came so far until I found the boat. And then the sea . . . We were so happy! All at once your ship—so fast—I could not get us out of the way!

(*Baby gurgles.*)

JUAN. She is so little, señor—so pretty. When she is afraid she never cry—just look at me like she say, "Brother, you take good care of me?"

(*Baby gurgles.*)

JUAN (*tearfully*). And I *will* take care of her, señor! I will! Give me a boat, señor! *Give me a boat!*

COMMANDANT (*repressed emotion in his voice*). All right, boy. It'll be all right. . . .

JUAN (*gulping*). Señor?

COMMANDANT. *This* is your boat. . . .

JUAN. Mine?

COMMANDANT. It'll take you to a place where—where, God willing, you and your sister will be safe.

JUAN (*unbelievingly*). You know such a place, señor?

COMMANDANT. Yes. . . . We are not so old there—we haven't forgotten that liberty is not a gift, but a victory. . . .

JUAN (*in close*). Look, señor, she has gone to sleep—my sister! It is because now she *knows* I can take care of her!

COMMANDANT (*down*). Take her outside, boy. The lieutenant will give you a place to sleep.

JUAN (*struggling with tears*). Gracia, señor! You are good. I—I thought there was no one left who was good. (*Fade*) Gracia. . . .

COMMANDANT. Sleep well, boy. . . .

(*Door back. Click of switch.*)

VOICE (*through communications system*). Radio room . . .

COMMANDANT. Make the following addition to message sent to flagship. Quote: in re skiff run down in fog. There were two survivors—a boy and a baby. We are proceeding on course. We are taking children—home.

(*Musical curtain.*)

AND ADAM BEGOT

Appeasement. Most people discovered the word for the first time when an ineffectual little man with an umbrella tried to make "peace in our time" with a man who signed a pact with one hand and reached for a gun with the other.

Appeasement is as old as human iniquity. Behind it hide all the world's ineffectuals, retreatists, best-of-all-possible worldists.

The network business is an appeasement business. Owning nothing but a nebulous nothingness consisting of contracts with radio stations who all sit under the constant threat of the Federal Communications Commission's axe, the networks pat all heads and rub all stomachs.

The only way to say what you must say on them is to learn the fine art of saying things by indirection.

When the Munich Pact turned my insides, I wanted to say what they *said could not be said over the air at the time, because we were a neutral nation*—they *said.*

So I went back to pre-Adam to say my piece: And Adam Begot.

AND ADAM BEGOT

ANNOUNCER. The place: the Dordogne region in the heart of France. At the side of a road simmering with the heat of a midsummer sun stands a large, dusty limousine. The engine tonneau is open and a begrimed little Frenchman tinkers at the engine. Within the limousine sit a young Englishwoman and Englishman. The woman laughs. . . .

KAY (*fade-in, laughingly*). Oh, poor Claude! Look at him! He's got enough engine grease over him to swim the Channel!

GEOFFREY (*cultured, quiet, young Englishman—an Embassy man*). He *is* rather a sight, isn't he?

KAY. Now that's a prize example of understatement, Geoffrey! Claude's not only a sight, he's a spectacle! The great Claude Renac nurse-maiding a balky engine in the middle of nowhere!

GEOFFREY. It was a mistake to have dismissed the chauffeur.

KAY. Oh, Claude'll have it running in a minute. He's very clever about machinery. (*Up*) Aren't you, Claude?

CLAUDE (*back—definite French accent*). Aren't I what, *ma chère?*

KAY (*up*). Aren't you clever with engines?

CLAUDE (*fade-in, close*). Ah, I think I will rest a moment and talk with you. This sun—it is doing its best to fry the little brains I have left.

KAY. You poor dear! Come—get in. Geoffrey was worried about your ability to fix the engine.

(*Sound of limousine door opening and closing.*)

49

CLAUDE (*sighs*). Ah! Most comfortable! You should try working with your hands, my dear Geoffrey—it gives one a most exquisite appreciation of the comforts of upholstered seats.

GEOFFREY (*stiffly*). Sorry I'm such a dud at machinery.

KAY. Now, now, Geoffrey, don't be so stuffy! Claude's much too primeval in his ways to be subtle. If he thought that you ought to help fix the engine, he'd be shouting the fact at the top of his voice!

CLAUDE (*chuckles*). Not at the top, my dear, but perhaps in the middle register. (*Sighs*) *Oui,* Kay, as usual you are right. I lack all knowledge of the diplomatic arts. If I do not like what a man is doing, I am forced to say so abruptly and completely! What an advantage you men of the diplomatic service have over we other poor mortals, my dear Geoffrey!

GEOFFREY. Sorry, but I'm much too warm at the moment to think you're very funny!

KAY (*laughingly*). Oh, you two! The minute you get together the great battle of words begins—aggressiveness versus diplomacy! The financier versus the diplomat! As the Americans say—bury the hatchet, my friends!

CLAUDE. Ah, I'm afraid Monsieur Wallace will never appreciate my virtues. He likes men who sit around green tables and talk. I, on the other hand, do not like sitting—I *do!*

GEOFFREY. The diplomatic way of getting things done is the only civilized way!

CLAUDE. And again, m'sieu, I must beg to disagree. There comes a time when, if a thing is to be done, one must *do* it and diplomacy—how you say it?—be hanged!

GEOFFREY. The philosophy of ruthlessness! Caveman philosophy!

CLAUDE. What do *we* know of cavemen?

GEOFFREY. I know that a ruthless aggressiveness may reap temporary rewards, but those rewards that have come in a far greater and more permanent form have resulted from the use of a civilized code—a friendly exchange, a calm consideration of fact—the ethical way of life.

CLAUDE (*scornfully*). The ethical way of life! I tell you, m'sieu . . .

KAY (*interrupting, laughingly*). All right, gentlemen, that's just about enough of that for one day!

GEOFFREY. So sorry!

CLAUDE. A thousand pardons, my dear Kay.

KAY. Now, then, Claudius, supposing you start diverting some of your aggression to that engine again?

CLAUDE. The engine? Oh, that—*fini!*

KAY. You mean it's fixed?

CLAUDE. But certainly!

KAY. The man is simply amazing! Let's be on our way—it's getting late!

GEOFFREY. Are you certain it will run, Renac?

CLAUDE. In my simplicity I know but one way to find out— and that is to try and start it!

(*Engine starter, engine catching and continuing under:*)

CLAUDE. *Voilà!*

KAY. Clever Claude! Isn't he, Geoffrey?

GEOFFREY (*flatly*). Let's hope it *continues* to run. . . .

KAY (*laughingly*). Charming thought! Let's be on our way, Claude, before we fall apart!

CLAUDE (*laughingly*). *Mais, certainement!*

(*Sound of automobile starting off; auto effects down and continuing far behind following:*)

KAY. We're very late, Claude, so speed is the word!

GEOFFREY. Right! The sooner we get out of this country the better I'll like it!

CLAUDE. Why do you say that?

GEOFFREY. I don't like this place—gives me the chills. . . .

KAY. With the sun doing its best to parboil us? What are you talking about?

GEOFFREY. I'm not talking of temperatures. I'm talking of—of —*atmospheres!* These forests and hills—whenever I travel through here I feel as if I were passing through a place old beyond decay!

CLAUDE. But that is amazing!

GEOFFREY. What do you mean?

CLAUDE. Because what you say of this country we are passing through—you speak profound truth!

KAY. Truth?

CLAUDE. We are at Le Moustier!

GEOFFREY (*repeats blankly*). Le Moustier?

CLAUDE. *Oui!* Does that mean nothing to you?

GEOFFREY. Nothing!

KAY. Nor to me, either!

CLAUDE. Le Moustier—the Mousterian Period! The dawn of mankind! The Neanderthal man!

GEOFFREY. Neand— You mean *here?*

CLAUDE. *Oui,* here—in this country which you say is old be- yond decay—were found Neanderthaloid skeletons. What you call cavemen—men from the dawn of man's antiquity!

KAY. Claude, are you serious?

CLAUDE. Yes—cavemen. Some place among these very rocks this road is climbing, five hundred centuries ago these men who were not quite men must have lived!

KAY. That's fascinating, Claude! Go on—tell us more!

GEOFFREY. It might be wiser to keep his eyes on the road.

CLAUDE (*a little testily*). Perhaps *you* would like to drive, my nervous friend?

KAY. Now, now! Go on, Claude—tell more about these cavemen of yours! You say they lived around here?

CLAUDE. Some of the finest specimens of Neanderthaloid skeletons have been discovered in the caves right in this region.

KAY. Really!

CLAUDE. It is unfortunate we are in such a hurry, or we could stop, perhaps, and see a few of the caves where the excavations have been made by the anthropologists.

GEOFFREY. We haven't time for that sort of thing!

CLAUDE (*irritably*). I said as much!

KAY (*admonishingly*). Claude!

CLAUDE. Your pardon! So, as I was saying, the anthropologists have found the most wonderful remains of this early species of man who are said to be the source of the horrible ogres in our fairy tales.

KAY (*laughingly*). What are you talking about?

CLAUDE. But I am most serious! The students of such matters have suggested that since the Neanderthal was extremely ugly—fierce expression—broad flat nose—great hairy arms and chest.

KAY. Ooo!

CLAUDE. It is quite possible that the memory of these beastmen may have remained in the minds of mankind all through the centuries until now we think that what is merely the hallucinations of dreams is really the memory of these monsters who wandered the earth in mankind's beginning.

GEOFFREY. Silly nonsense!

KAY. Yes, Claude, how could anyone possibly know after fifty thousand years what this Neanderthal caveman looked like?

CLAUDE. But that is simple! From the peculiarities of the skeletons that have been found it is simple to reconstruct the physical appearance of the race!

KAY. Really?

CLAUDE. I remember hearing the hands and feet were very large—the thigh bones curved, so that the men walked like apes. . . .

GEOFFREY. Bah!

CLAUDE (*going right on*). Teeth and jaws were large—yes, and enormous brow ridges resulting in a fierce horrible expression!

KAY. How nice!

GEOFFREY. How long does this lecture go on?

CLAUDE. The brain capacity of the skulls that have been found is very small, so it is believed that the Neanderthaler had a very different mentality from ours. The back parts of the brain which deal with sight and touch, with the quickness and energy of the body, were well developed, but the front parts connected with thought and speech—ah, that was another story! They were men and not men—horrible caricatures of . . .

GEOFFREY (*interrupting*). Kay, would you mind telling your erudite friend to step on the accelerator? We've got to be at Monet within two hours! We'll never get there at the pace he's driving!

CLAUDE. And, Kay, would you tell your impatient compatriot that I drive as fast and in the manner that pleases me alone! Would you tell him that . . .

KAY (*up in great fright*). Claude! Look out! The road's blocked!

(*Sound of squealing brakes.*)

GEOFFREY. Don't swing your wheel! The cliff!

CLAUDE. The steering gear! Something is wrong! I can't . . .

KAY (*in great chilling horror*). *The cliff!*

(*Music: through the rising music we hear screams fading quickly, then a crash far back as the automobile hits the rocks far below. The music rises and covers the scene.*)

KAY (*pleadingly—from her voice it is obvious that she has just gone through a horrible experience*). Geoffrey! Geoffrey, please—open your eyes!

(GEOFFREY *groans.*)

KAY (*tearful note in voice*). Geoffrey, please—open your eyes! I am so frightened! I . . .

GEOFFREY (*weakly*). Kay. . . .

KAY. Oh, thank God, you're all right!

GEOFFREY (*weakly*). You—you're all right?

KAY. Yes, yes, I'm all right! But Claude—I—I don't know where he is!

GEOFFREY. The cliff—we went over . . .

KAY. We were thrown clear, I guess. The car's over there. I see it all broken up. But Claude—I can't see him!

GEOFFREY. Help me up . . . (*Cries out in pain*) Ah!

KAY (*in quick response*). What—

GEOFFREY. My arm—broken, I guess.

KAY. Oh, Geoffrey!

GEOFFREY (*in pain*). I'll be all right—lucky to be alive!

KAY. I don't understand—going over that horrible cliff! And —Claude! Oh, Geoffrey, where's Claude?

GEOFFREY. Brush so thick here—we'll have to look . . .

CLAUDE (*far back, calling*). Kay! Geoffrey! Where are you?

KAY (*happily*). It's Claude! (*Up*) Claude! We're here! Where are you?

CLAUDE (*back*). Back here! In the brush!

GEOFFREY (*up*). Come ahead! What's the matter—are you hurt?

CLAUDE (*back*). My knee! Kay, are you all right?

KAY (*up*). Yes, Claude! All right! Stay where you are! We'll come to you! (*Fade*) We'll come to you! Don't move!

(*Transitional short pause.*)

CLAUDE (*cries out in great pain*). Ahhhh!

KAY. Sorry, Claude. I've got to get that knee bandaged.

CLAUDE (*one gets the impression that he is speaking through clenched teeth*). It is all right. . . . A little pain is better than permanent oblivion. . . . (*In pain*) Ahh!

GEOFFREY. Sorry I can't be of help, old man. (*From his voice it is apparent he is in pain too*) This blasted arm of mine!

CLAUDE. It is all right, my friend. Kay is doing—excellently. . . .

KAY. There we are! Snug as a bug! How does that feel?

CLAUDE. The great Florence Nightingale could have done no better! I kiss your hand!

KAY (*not too much fun in her voice*). For a man who just escaped from a horrible death you're doing quite well!

GEOFFREY. Death. . . . The trees and bushes broke our fall, but the wonder is that we weren't killed! Look at the cliff! Falling that terrific distance . . . And you, Kay, not hurt at all—it's a miracle!

CLAUDE (*seriously*). Mais, oui—miracle . . .

(*Wind sighs, and continues to rise and fall intermittently behind following scene.*)

KAY. How—cold it is!

CLAUDE. *Oui!* That wind!

KAY. Freezing!

GEOFFREY. But how could that be? It's the middle of July!

KAY. Claude—Geoffrey—what is this? The car goes over a

cliff—we don't die. A warm sunny day, and now suddenly it's like winter! (*Hysterical note coming into voice*) What is this? Tell me! What is this?

GEOFFREY. Steady, Kay!

CLAUDE. *Oui,* there must be some logical explanation! I know this country like you say—like the back of my hand! There is never such cold wind here in July! I tell you . . . (*In pain*) Ahhh!

KAY. Oh, Claude! You shouldn't try to get up!

CLAUDE. I—I am all right!

GEOFFREY. Got to get help somehow!

CLAUDE. No, no—all I want now—is a cigarette. . . .

GEOFFREY. I haven't any—there are some in the side pocket of the car. I'll get . . .

KAY. No, Geoffrey, I'll get them!

GEOFFREY. But . . .

KAY. You can't get through the bushes with that arm of yours! I'm all right! (*Fade*) I'll be right back. . . .

CLAUDE (*up*). Kay!

GEOFFREY. Kay, wait!

KAY (*far back*). I'll be back in a minute!

(*Wind sighs.*)

CLAUDE. This infernal knee!

GEOFFREY. Better sit quietly. . . .

CLAUDE. Quietly! Quietly! It is not in my nature to be quiet! A stick—get me a stick! I am not going to lie here the rest of my life! Get me a stick for a crutch and I'll . . .

GEOFFREY (*excitedly*). Wait, old man.

CLAUDE. But, I tell you . . .

GEOFFREY. Wait, I tell you! There's someone coming!

CLAUDE. Kay?

GEOFFREY. No, no! The other direction.

CLAUDE. But I do not see . . .

GEOFFREY. Over there to the right! Don't you see—bushes being shoved back . . .

CLAUDE. Yes, I see! Some peasant who will give us assistance! *Oui,* now everything will be all right.

GEOFFREY. Of course! There! He's in the clearing! Now he . . .

CLAUDE (*cries out in great surprise*). Ahh!

GEOFFREY (*in mingled awe and horror, in close*). Who—who is *that?*

CLAUDE (*softly*). Oh, no!

GEOFFREY (*hoarsely*). Claude! Who?

CLAUDE. Am I mad? This cannot be!

GEOFFREY. He—he's looking at *me!*

(*Wind sighs.*)

CLAUDE. Gone!

GEOFFREY. Yes! But—but who?

CLAUDE (*slowly*). Who? You do not understand?

GEOFFREY (*impatiently*). Understand what? Talk up?

CLAUDE. Did you not see him as I saw him? The short, hairy, twisted body? The head thrust forward—the neck bent like an ape—those enormous brow ridges—the broad flat nose? You did not recognize?

GEOFFREY. Well? *Well?*

CLAUDE (*in close*). Once—in your own British Museum, I saw a reproduction of a man like that! But never did I think that I would see him in life!

GEOFFREY. I tell you, speak! Who was he?

CLAUDE. A man of the caves—a Neanderthaler!

GEOFFREY (*blankly*). Neander— Are you insane? The race is extinct fifty thousand years!

CLAUDE. I tell you only what I saw, what I *know!*

GEOFFREY. And I tell you, you're mad!

CLAUDE. But you saw as I did! The thick, hairy body! The short, ape-like limbs! That misshapen face like something out of a nightmare! Yes, a nightmare of fifty thousand years ago! (*Wind*) A caveman comes out of the past to . . .

GEOFFREY (*interrupting angrily*). No, no! Stop talking like that! It can't be! I tell you it can't! He's some madman wandering these forests, that's all! Cavemen died here fifty thousand years ago! The past doesn't turn back! I tell you, it doesn't! We . . . (*Stops abruptly, then down intensely*) Claude!

(*Wind sighs.*)

CLAUDE. Eh?

GEOFFREY (*down, intensely*). Kay!

CLAUDE (*gasps*). Ah!

GEOFFREY (*calling*). Kay! Kay! Where are you? (*Ad lib, continuing.*)

CLAUDE (*joins him*). Kay! Kay! Where are you? Answer! Kay! Kay!

(*Music rises and covers their cries, then fades out behind. Sound of men fighting their way through heavy brush.*)

GEOFFREY (*fade-in, impatiently*). Hurry, Renac! Faster, faster! We've got to find her while there is still daylight!

CLAUDE (*wearily*). I am sorry, my dear Geoffrey—but this branch—it makes a very poor substitute for a crutch.

GEOFFREY (*mechanically, as if good breeding is speaking rather than immediate interest in* CLAUDE's *plight*). Sorry, old man! Let me help you!

CLAUDE. No, no, it is quite all right—I can manage.

GEOFFREY. You should have waited back there.

CLAUDE. I would rather die in an attempt to do something than lie on my back like a worm in the dirt!

GEOFFREY. What are you talking about?

CLAUDE. Kay!

GEOFFREY. Eh?

CLAUDE. If I remember my Palaeolithic Age history, there should be saber-toothed tigers and cave-bears, and cave-lions and other such animals wandering about. . . .

GEOFFREY (*irritably*). Are you still raving that time has turned back?

CLAUDE. I believe the evidence of my eyes!

GEOFFREY. It's nonsense! I tell you—hallucination!

CLAUDE. Eh?

GEOFFREY. Yes, yes, hallucination! Driving along we were talking about the Neanderthal men, so when we saw that huge hairy peasant we immediately took for granted that here was one of the Neanderthal come to life! I tell you the air was hazy—our nerves are shot! We saw things that don't exist!

CLAUDE. Why is it so bitter cold? *That,* at least, is reality?

GEOFFREY. Keep moving!

CLAUDE. So I'll answer my own question—it is bitter cold because time has moved back to the third inter-glacial age. . . .

GEOFFREY (*snorts in disgust*). Aww!

CLAUDE. You do not believe the evidence of your senses, yet perhaps you will believe that is a campfire up ahead?

GEOFFREY (*sharply*). Where?

CLAUDE. Far ahead—where those hills are white . . .

GEOFFREY. It is a fire! Quickly, Renac! Can't you hobble faster? Kay—we'll get whoever's there to help us find Kay! (*Fade*) Hurry, Renac—hurry—hurry . . . !

(*Transitional short pause, then fade-in sound of wind blowing, down and continuing far behind.*)

GEOFFREY (*awe in his voice*). It's—it's the one we saw all right!

CLAUDE (*hoarsely, sotto*). Keep your voice down! He will hear us!

GEOFFREY (*sotto, hoarsely*). What—what manner of man *is* he?

CLAUDE. Time and time again I have told you!

GEOFFREY. But he and all like him have been dead fifty thousand years! You said that yourself! And the dead don't come to life!

CLAUDE. *We* have come into *his* life—not *he* into ours!

GEOFFREY. Kay!

CLAUDE. Keep your voice down!

GEOFFREY. But Kay . . .

CLAUDE. She is not there—you can see for yourself!

GEOFFREY. Then she's lost—wandering around . . .

CLAUDE. Keep your voice down! I warn you!

GEOFFREY. Eh?

CLAUDE. His senses must be keen as an animal's!

GEOFFREY. Look—he is getting to his feet!

CLAUDE. *Mon Dieu,* if I had a gun!

GEOFFREY. Come on—we'll get up—we'll talk to him!

CLAUDE. Talk?

GEOFFREY. Lunatic—savage—whatever he is—perhaps he's seen Kay!

CLAUDE. Get down, you fool!

GEOFFREY. No! I'm going to talk to him!

CLAUDE. Stay down! Geoffrey!

GEOFFREY (*up*). Hey, you up there! Look! We want to talk to you!

CLAUDE (*hopelessly*). You fool, you fool, what have you done?

GEOFFREY (*confidently*). There! He's coming this way! Now I'll settle this!

CLAUDE (*hopelessly*). Oh, you! While we were unseen we had a chance to plan—to do! But now—now . . .

GEOFFREY. Don't talk like that! I was in West Africa for two years! I know how to deal with savages!

CLAUDE. Look at him! You think that is even a—a savage?

GEOFFREY. Huh! He's stopped! Afraid of us! Gad, he's the ugliest beggar I've ever seen! (*Up*) I say there, old man! Come closer! We're friends! See—friends! (*Aside to* CLAUDE) Smile, Renac! Show him we're friends! Smile!

CLAUDE. Unimaginative fool—we need an automatic pistol, not a smile!

GEOFFREY. See, he's coming closer! He sees we mean no harm!

CLAUDE. He sees we are harmless! Against the strength in those arms . . .

GEOFFREY. Stop talking like that! I'll meet him half way—he'll listen to me. (*Up*) Friends, old man! Friends (*Fade slowly*) Money! I bring you money! Pretty things!

CLAUDE (*disgustedly*). *Mon Dieu,* what a fool! Words and money for *him!* (*Up in sudden alarm*) Geoffrey! Look out!

(*Animal-like sounds of caveman back, deep-throated monosyllables—continuing behind.*)

GEOFFREY (*back—struggling*). Let me go! Let me go! You! Friends—hear me—friends! Put me down! Put me down! (*Fade*) Put me down!

(*Music rises and covers his struggle, then fades out behind.*)

CLAUDE (*from the strain in his voice it is apparent that he, too, is in great agony*). Do not—do not try to hold back your tears, my friend. . . .

GEOFFREY. That devil . . .

CLAUDE. I never realized before what pain the human mind could endure. . . .

GEOFFREY. Why did he do this to me? Why?

CLAUDE. Do you ask the wolf why it kills?

GEOFFREY. Killing would be one thing, but . . .

CLAUDE. Once I saw a gypsy break the wings of a wild bird. . . .

GEOFFREY. Renac!

CLAUDE. Memory is strange. Before my eyes I see so clearly a book I read—oh, many years ago. It said that perhaps the men of the caves—the men of Neanderthal—found existence so difficult, food in a cold bitter world so hard to get, that they ate—what all men should abhor. . . .

GEOFFREY. Renac! What of Kay?

CLAUDE. *Oui,* I have been thinking of Kay. . . . When the horrible pain in my bones lets me think. All through the night . . .

GEOFFREY. He hasn't . . .

CLAUDE (*wearily*). Who knows—who knows? The mouth of the cave . . . If I could only twist around so I could see . . . (*Gasps*) *Mon Dieu*—the pain!

GEOFFREY. I never thought the time would come in my life when I couldn't reason something out. . . . This is beyond reason! Broken bones—thrown into a cave like a side of beef to wait—to wait for what—what . . . ? If I only . . .

CLAUDE (*interrupting sharply*). Wait! Wait!

GEOFFREY. Wha' . . .

CLAUDE. Someone is coming. I heard . . .

GEOFFREY. I hear nothing!

CLAUDE. Listen!

(KAY *sobbing, back, fade-in slowly, beginning at "I hear nothing."*)

CLAUDE. A woman! (*Up, whispering hoarsely*) Kay!

GEOFFREY. Katherine, is it you?

CLAUDE. Kay! Answer!

KAY (*in full, weepily*). Oh, Geoffrey! Claude!

GEOFFREY. Kay, *you!*

CLAUDE. Kay!

GEOFFREY. Oh, Katherine, are you all right?

CLAUDE. Kay! Where were you?

KAY. No, no, *you*—are both of you all right?

GEOFFREY. We—we're all right!

CLAUDE. We don't matter. You—are you . . . ?

KAY. So dark in here! Are you all right—tell me!

GEOFFREY. Katherine, you . . .

CLAUDE. It is you that matters! What . . . ?

KAY. Oh, no, listen—there's so little time!

CLAUDE. Eh?

GEOFFREY. Wha' . . .

KAY. He's busy building up the fire. There's a chance if we run quickly!

CLAUDE (*bitterly*). Run quickly. . . .

KAY. Yes! Come!

GEOFFREY (*in pain*). We—are not at liberty—to go, my dear. . . .

KAY. *Why?*

CLAUDE. A matter of—broken bones . . .

KAY (*down, tensely*). Oh, no. . . .

CLAUDE. That's the way it is. . . .

KAY (*quickly, tensely*). Tell me—what happened? Geoffrey, you— Claude, you—tell me what happened to us? That old . . . Who is he? Is he really a Neanderthal . . . ?

CLAUDE. There is no doubt. . . .

KAY. But men like that have been dead for centuries! How did it happen? Why are we here?

GEOFFREY. Yes, why are we here? How could *we* get into the *past?*

CLAUDE. There is but one explanation—and, insane and impossible as it is, it is the only explanation!

KAY. Tell me!

CLAUDE. When the automobile went over the cliff, we went into another dimension of time!

GEOFFREY. Wha-at?

KAY. I don't understand!

CLAUDE. And I, too, understand little, but can it be that events in time are static things? That everything which occurs remains in existence as life moves on further along the—the corridor of time?

KAY. Then you mean when the automobile went over the cliff, in some way we went *back* into time instead of *forward?*

CLAUDE. *Oui!*

GEOFFREY. No, no, that's impossible! Things exist when they exist, not afterwards! There's a factual explanation to all this!

CLAUDE (*sardonically*). Factual? Is not the pain of our bones fact enough? Is not . . . ?

(*Beginning at "Is not the pain" in above speech, we hear the hoarse semi-human chant of the caveman far back, continuing far behind:*)

KAY. Wait!

GEOFFREY. What is it?

CLAUDE. A chant of some sort!

KAY. Why is he . . . ?

65

(*Chant in a little.*)

GEOFFREY. What is he saying? What?

CLAUDE (*sotto*). The beginning of worship . . . The chant to the rising sun. . . .

KAY (*slowly, suggestion of tears in her voice*). What—is happening—to us? Only a few hours ago—so happy—the three of us—on our way to a party . . .

CLAUDE. Parties . . . Another age . . .

GEOFFREY. We've got to *do* something!

CLAUDE (*after pause*). Strange . . .

KAY. What?

CLAUDE. Only a few hours ago *I* was the doer and you, Geoffrey, the calm, poised diplomat of the green tables. . . .

(*Chanting begins to fade-in slowly.*)

GEOFFREY. Stop talking nonsense! Listen! He's coming in here! For us! We've got to do something! Do you hear me —do something! I won't die! I can't die! Do something! Do you hear me? Do something? I won't die like this! I won't! I'll . . .

CLAUDE (*interrupting sharply*). Geoffrey!

GEOFFREY (*takes a deep shuddering breath*). Sorry. I never could endure pain. . . .

CLAUDE. We understand, Geoffrey. . . .

KAY. Try not to think, dear. . . .

GEOFFREY. All my life I've—I've known what to say—and now . . .

KAY. Geoffrey, don't . . .

GEOFFREY. No, let me talk—while I can talk I'm a man—and I won't be a man when *he* gets in here!

CLAUDE. If I had a gun. . . .

GEOFFREY. A world of reason—that's what it was to me! And

66

everything could be settled with reason in a world of reason!

CLAUDE. If I had a gun. . . .

GEOFFREY. Everything could be straightened out at the conference table. Yes, that's what I thought! All my life it would be that way. All my life. You see, that was because I'd never met *force* in all my life!

CLAUDE. If I had a gun. . . .

GEOFFREY. But you can't reason with *unreason*, can you? When you're facing brute force, words and ethics and logic and good faith don't mean anything, do they?

CLAUDE. If I had a gun!

GEOFFREY. You've got to face force with force—and a gun is force, and I've *got* a gun!

KAY. Geoffrey!

CLAUDE. He's out of his head!

GEOFFREY. Yes, yes, I tell you I've got a gun! Diplomatic service—they made me carry it! I hated it, I thought I'd never use it, but now we've got to, don't we? We've *got* to!

(*Chanting coming in closer.*)

KAY (*cries out sharply*). Ah! He's coming in here!

GEOFFREY. Claude, *your* right arm's all right! My pocket— there—the gun! Take it! Use it!

CLAUDE. But I—I . . .

GEOFFREY. Use it! If we're to live, use it!

(*Chanting is in very close—the beast is almost on them.*)

KAY. Geoffrey! It's reaching . . .

GEOFFREY. Claude!

CLAUDE. No, I—I—my hands—I—I can't . . .

GEOFFREY. Then *I'll* stop him!

(*Shot in close.*)

(*The chanting cuts off sharply with shot—heavy thud, back.*)

67

CLAUDE (*deep shuddering breath, then:*) So. . . .

(*Wind sighs.*)

KAY (*slowly*). It's—morning. . . .

CLAUDE. *Oui.* . . .

KAY. Now. . . .

CLAUDE. We go on living. . . . Something may happen to re- .
turn us to where we belong. . . .

KAY. I—don't—think so. . . .

CLAUDE. Nor I. Perhaps we will be able to leave some record
behind us, so that the world of the future will know and
understand this strange thing that has happened. . . . This
meeting of the present and the past . . .

(*Wind sighs.*)

KAY. Geoffrey—don't—just stare. . . . It's over. . . . Talk to
us. . . .

GEOFFREY (*slowly*). I was thinking. . . . I just killed a man
—yet it's fifty thousand years before I was born!

(*Musical curtain.*)

DARK WORLD

There is a national illusion that "stars are difficult to work with." The canard was begun, undoubtedly, by awestricken pseudo-directors who found in the alleged temperament of the performers an excuse for personal shortcomings.

Don't get the idea that Davis or Laughton or Crawford or Bergner or Shearer are mothers' little helpmates; with their accumulated two hundred centuries of perception, they recognize phony direction or phony material faster than the time it takes for light to travel between two moons on the left-hand side of Saturn.

But give them a play they can sink their creative teeth into, or give them direction that respects a mutual minimum of intelligence, and they work you and themselves until you wish that you had listened to mother and married into that critic's family.

DARK WORLD

(*Music: Down and out behind.*)

ANNOUNCER. The scene: a hospital room. A nurse stands writing on a chart. . . .

(*Sound: Fade-in scratching of pen on paper together with:*)

MARGE (*slowly, as she writes*). Died—2 A.M. . . .

AMY (*tensely*). Marge! Let's get out of here!

MARGE. What in the world are you . . . ?

AMY. Can't you hear me? Let's get out of here!

MARGE. Amy! What's the matter with you?

AMY (*tensely*). Nothing! Nothing. . . .

MARGE. Then let me finish the report! Uh . . .

(*Sound: Pen scratching behind:*)

MARGE. Died—2 A.M. Miss Carol.

AMY (*sharply*). No, no, stop it!

MARGE. Amy!

AMY (*begins to cry*). Oh, Marge!

MARGE. Amy, stop that!

AMY (*weepily*). I—I can't help it!

MARGE. If Doctor Ellis comes back—what'll he . . . ?

AMY. I don't care! I don't care! Oh, why did she die? *Why?*

MARGE. I—I just don't get it! All the time you've been on the staff, I've never seen you act this way over losing a case! And especially this one—blind—paralyzed—helpless . . .

AMY. That's just it! For twenty-five years—from the hour she was born—Carol Mathews had nothing but loneliness and misery! And then to die like this—never having known anything but darkness—it isn't fair—it isn't fair!

71

MARGE (*softly*). She—she liked you, didn't she, Amy?

AMY. Yes, I think she did. . . . When I'd come into the room, she always seemed to know. She'd turn her face toward the door and she'd say softly, "Hello, Amy. . . . (*Fade*) Hello, Amy. . . ."

(*Fade-in "Swan of Tuonela," fading back after a few seconds behind.*)

CAROL (*in close, softly*). Hello, Amy. . . . Hello, Amy . . . No, you can't hear me, can you? And yet I must speak—while I'm still here close to you. You said I'd never known anything but darkness. . . . You're very wrong, Amy. There was never any darkness in my world. How could there be? The skies that I saw never clouded. The flowers never faded. The trees were always green and fresh. I saw a lovely world in my darkness, Amy—lovely. . . .

(*Music: Fades out.*)

AMY (*fade-in fast*). And just think, Marge—all those years in bed! Never moving . . . Nothing happening—day after day after day! If she'd had *my* eyes—if she could have moved around like *I* do—the world would have been hers! (*Fade*) I tell you the world would have been hers!

(*Music: in with:*)

CAROL. The world, Amy? Why do you want to give me what I've already had? I had so much! Yes, lying there—I had the world! Don't you remember? *You* gave it to me! Hugo and Conrad, and all the rest—theirs weren't just words printed on white pages as you read them to me! They were white, flaming magic that carried me so far away from here—to the sea. . . . (*At "to the sea," fade-in the roar of the sea and wind and hold far, far back behind following:*) The wind—the hurricane—man fighting for life . . . I tell you, I was there! *I was there!* (*Background cuts out knife-*

clean at her final "I was there!") Nothing happening? Oh, Amy, have you forgotten Charles Dickens? Paris—the roar of the streets in the Revolution? (*Fade-in the roar of the mob at "Paris" and hold far, far back behind*) Crowds—pushing, fighting all around me. An old world dying—a new one struggling its way up through blood—and I was there, Amy! *I was there!* (*Background of mob out knife-clean at final "I was there!"*) Yes, whatever you read to me, Amy—wherever the place or whatever the time—the past or the future, the jungle or the Arctic—(*Building*) that's where I was, Amy! *That's where I was!* (*Softly*) How could you forget?

(*Music: Fade-out.*)

AMY (*fade-in*). And that's why it's so terribly unfair, Marge. She never saw anything—*anything!* If she even had a few years when she could have seen things—the—the world! But to—go away and never have seen things as they really were—(*Fade*) what a terrible thing, Marge!

("*Swan of Tuonela,*" *behind.*)

CAROL. Things as they really were, Amy? Would it have been so wonderful to see things as they were? (*Sound: Fade-in sound of marching feet*) Men marching again, with death at their shoulders. . . . (*Sound: Marching feet up, and then out behind*) Marching, to give *death* to all that other men had struggled for centuries to give *life*? (*Sound: Jeering mob, back*) Death for human rights. . . .

(*Sound: Mob up, then fade-out.*)

DICTATOR (*fade-in*). Democracy is an illusion! Democracy is the dictum of cattle! We laugh at freedom! (*Fade*) All for the state! All for the state!

CAROL. Death to the freedom of the human soul. . . .

DICTATOR (*fade-in*). Ours is a holy cause! The truth is the truth only when it furthers that holy cause! (*Fade*) The lie is the truth when it makes the masses believe!

CAROL. Death to honor!

DICTATOR (*fade-in*). The democracies dare not resist! They cannot! Weaken them from within and then to save them from (*Fade*) themselves we will strike and make them our people!

(*Sound: Whistle of falling bomb followed by screams of people, fading slowly behind.*)

CAROL. Things as they *were*, Amy . . . Would there have been happiness for me in that? No. In my wonderful darkness—things as they *could* be—I had that. A world of space and freedom, where each man had a dignity of self so great that he could not bear the hurt of other men who are all as himself. Men who know that freedom was never a gift—but always a victory. Things as they were, Amy? No—things as they *must* be. . . .

(*Music: Out.*)

AMY (*fade-in fast*). And, Marge, she must have been very lonely. No one ever coming to visit her. No one in the world who cared if she lived or died—so lonely—(*Fade*) so lonely.

(*Music: In behind.*)

CAROL. Lonely? Oh, Amy, didn't you ever understand about my friends? They were the greatest friends a woman ever had. I chose them from the good and the great! They used to come into this room—yes, and sit by me and talk to me! (*Sound: People, back, talking, laughing behind*) The Brownings—oh, such charming people—and Shakespeare—I used to argue with him! And Keats . . . (*Sound: People fade-out*) And Walt Whitman—yes, he was here, too. . . .

He taught me not to be afraid! Don't you remember how he said:

MALE VOICE (*in close*). I was thinking the day most splendid, till I saw the night. I was thinking this globe enough, till there sprang out so noiseless around me myriads of other globes!

CAROL. Lonely! Oh, my dear! Was ever a woman more fortunate than I? The box that stood beside the bed . . . You talked of playing records—but again it was a visit from my friends! (*Music: Piano playing "Moonlight Sonata" far back*) Beethoven, here in my room—when I was weary. He'd play so softly, with tired fingers . . . Here, I tell you . . . And I'd know it was for me. . . . (*Music: Piano up, then out. Fade-in "Swan of Tuonela"*) And Schubert and Brahms and Mozart and Tschaikowsky—all of them—my friends! Lonely? (*Vibrantly*) No, Amy! The days weren't long enough!

(*Music: Out.*)

AMY (*fade-in fast*). And she was beautiful! So very beautiful! I—I don't know exactly how to say it, but she was like a flower hidden away in a dark forest! Every time I'd go out with Joe, I used to think of her lying here more beautiful than anyone I'd ever known—and she had no one. (*Fade*) No one. . . .

(*"Swan of Tuonela" behind.*)

CAROL. No one, Amy? There *was* someone. His name? He didn't have a name, but he was there when I was weary and needed him. . . . Yes, you had your Joe, Amy, but in your heart I knew there was someone else—someone *you* had dreamed of—someone you'd never meet, perhaps—someone you'd forget as all women forget when they marry their Joes. But I didn't have to forget the one in my heart, Amy. He was real to me—as real as my friends that came to me with their words and music whenever I stretched out my hand— as real as that lovely world that was mine alone. . . . A dream world, Amy? What are dreams? (*Music: Out at "Mine alone"*) What is real and unreal? We see only what we want to see. . . . I made a world in my darkness where everyone walked in loveliness—where things were as they might some day be. . . . (*Music: Begins to fade-in slowly playing the finale of Goddard's "Adagio Pathetique"*) It's almost time, Amy . . .

MAN's VOICE (*far back—calling—echo*). Carol!

CAROL (*happily*). Yes, I hear you! Yes. . . . I must move on, Amy. Thank you for your pity—but pity is for those who have nothing—and I had a world where all was beauty. . . . Yes, Amy, believe me (*In close*) I was *very* happy. . . . (*Musical curtain.*)

GENGHIS KHAN

I had always had an idea that the network censor was tall and gaunt and looked something like John Carradine—with the difference that the network censor drooled a little and slept in a bed whose corner posts were shaped like phallic symbols.

Then, finally, one Octember day, I actually met some of those guardians of the kilocycle purity, and I found them very hard-working, position-conscious ladies and gentlemen with a difficult, vaguely outlined job to do—which, miraculously, they did.

Particularly difficult was the position of this "continuity-acceptance" department during the time of America's "neutrality" to the second European horror.

Since the wisest move a corporation can make under any unusual circumstance is to play safe, an order came down from that little god who sits on top of the corporation's topmost salary bracket, that, until further notice, the war was to be ignored by the radio dramatists. In other words, with one swoop of an inter-office memo, the network abolished reality.

But memos couldn't abolish the actuality of the horror, and one was torn day after day by the personal conviction that the fight was our fight, and that to wait until the enemy chose his time was to wait a tragic moment too late.

One had to speak, but that neutrality memo stood between one's typewriter and the microphones. Again one had to take the indirect path—and so Genghis Khan.

GENGHIS KHAN

(*Music: Down behind.*)

VOICE (*slowly, portentously*). . . . and so, in the desert of
Asia, there arose a man—Temujin—him the Tartars called
Genghis Khan, the greatest of warriors, ruler of men! And
he gathered about him the hordes of the Mongols, and he
swept down on Cathay and Russia and plundered and destroyed, pillaged and burned—cruel beyond all understanding—for he believed himself divinely inspired to conquer
the world. Yes, he was the mightiest of those who ruled
with fire and blood and sword and hatred, but he, too, died,
and his body was buried under a great tree that bent in
the wailing wind. . . .

(*Music up as transition, then out behind—sound of city street
back behind.*)

MAE (*a Harlem Negress in her late twenties, well on the way
to shrewdom*). Sam! Ya good for nuthin'! How many
times I gotta tell ya to shut dat dah window! Shut it, I
tell ya!

SAM (*he is large and simple and easy-going*). All right! All
right!

(*Sound of window closing; street noises down and almost out,
slowly fading out behind the following:*)

SAM (*grumbling*). No good, dat's what it is!

MAE (*fade-in full*). What's dat you say?

SAM. I said it's no good!

MAE (*laughs shortly*). Scared, dat's what ya is!

SAM. I ain't!

MAE (*tauntingly*). Sam—ole house-painter Sam—so scared his ears are goin' flop-flop!

SAM. Don't ya talk like dat!

MAE. What ya scared about?

SAM. I ain't scared! But I'm sayin' dat dere's things dat ya better leave alone!

MAE. Aw, let mamma have her fun! She ain't gonna conjure nuthin' up!

SAM. Den what she wanna mess around for wid dat spirit talk?

MAE. Huh! Ah declare, Sam, you's de biggest man in all Harlem, an' you's got de smallest brain!

SAM. Sez you!

MAE. Sez me! She's an ole lady my mamma is! So I sez let her have her fun! If she wanna turn off de light an' say dem funny words an' try to conjure up de spirits, I sez let her! Don't do no harm . . .

SAM. Dat's what you say!

MAE. Yeah, dat's what Ah say! She'll wave her hands an' call on de spirits an' de spirits won't come an' dat's all dere'll be to it!

SAM (*disgustedly*). Yeah!

MAE. Aw, now, Sam . . .

MOTHER (*back, calling; she has an old cracked voice*). Mae! I'se waitin' for ya!

MAE (*up*). Be dere in a minute, Mamma!

MOTHER (*back as before*). An' bring dat man of yourn in!

MAE (*up*). Yeah, be dere in a minute, Mamma! Now, come along, Sam—she's waitin'!

SAM (*grumbling*). Ain't gonna do it!

MAE. Oh, yes, you is! Ya don't go in dere, den mamma she's gonna be so mad dere ain't gonna be no livin' in dis place fo' a week! Now ya know how my mamma gets when she's sore!

SAM (*disgustedly*). Yeah!

MAE. Ya come along now! (*Scornfully*) *Big* Sam! Yeah! *Baby* Sam!

SAM. Now, ya ain't got no call to talk like dat, Mae!

MAE. Den come along!

MOTHER (*back, calling impatiently*). Mae! Is you comin' in here?

MAE. Yeah, Mamma, here we come! (*Sotto*) Now, come along, Sam, come along!

(*Sound of walking along hallway.*)

SAM (*reluctantly*). Aw . . .

MAE (*pleased*). Dat's my sweet man!

SAM (*grumbling*). Ain't no good gonna come of it, nohow!

MAE (*scornfully*). Aw!

(*Sound of opening door; walking sound out.*)

MOTHER (*in a little closer*). Come on in! Come on in! Ah's waitin' for ya!

MAE. Dat's all right, Mamma. We's here.

MOTHER (*back as before*). Shut de door! Shut de door!

(*Closing door.*)

MOTHER. Now, Sam, you go turn off de light!

SAM (*reluctantly*). Now, look here, ole lady . . .

MOTHER (*up, in senile anger of the old*). Turn off de light! Ah said! Turn 'em off!

MAE (*sharply*). Sam!

SAM (*fading*). Okay! Okay!

MOTHER. Big good-for-nuthin' loafer!

(*Snap of switch.*)

MOTHER. Now, ya come back here, Sam, an' sit down in dat dere chair! No, dat one, ya fool! You, Mae . . .

MAE. Yes, Mamma?

MOTHER. Ya sit dere! Now both of ya put your hands on de table! Ah gotta conjure up de spirits!

SAM (*grumbling*). Whatta ya gotta do dat fo'?

MOTHER (*sharply*). What's dat you say?

SAM (*reluctantly*). Ah—Ah just said whatta ya wanna conjure up de spirits fo'?

MOTHER. You're a fool man, dat's what ya is! (*Scornfully*) What Ah wanna conjure up spirits fo'? 'Cause Ah had a dream, dat's why!

MAE. Yeah, dat's de truth!

MOTHER. A dream—plain as de nose on yah face! A dream dat Ah conjured up spirits right in dis here room! De most wonderful spirits as ever was!

SAM. Don' like it!

MOTHER. Who cares what ya like, ya big hunk o' nuthin'? Who cares what ya like? Now shut your face an' lemme conjure!

MAE (*eagerly*). Go ahead, Mamma!

MOTHER. Shh! (*Mystically*) Spirits o' de dark—lissen to me! It's me—Liz Johnson talkin'. Spirits o' de dark—here in mah hand Ah hold de dried blood of a black rooster! With it Ah mixes de toad oil and de cat's tongue an' Ah calls on ya, spirits! Come forth out o' de darkness an' bring me all de good news dat Ah wanna hear! Awake, O' mighty spirits, an' take mah offerin'! In a dream Ah saw ya, an' Ah knows ya come fo' me dis night! (*Up*) Ah conjures ya up, spirits! Up, spirits! Spirits, Ah conjures ya!

(*For a few seconds all that is heard is the heavy breathing of the three people, then:*)

SAM. Ain't nuthin'. . . .

MOTHER (*angrily*). Ya did it! Ya did it! Ya broke de spell!

SAM. Ah didn't do nuthin'! Ah . . .

MOTHER. Broke de spell, ya did! Jes' when de spirits was a-risin'! No-good fool!

MAE. But, Mother, Sam . . .

MOTHER. Turn on de lights! Throw up de blinds! Nuthin' ain't no good! Conjure's broke! Turn on de lights!

(*Click of electric switch.*)

MAE (*fade-in*). Dere ya are, Mamma—de lights! (*Tensely*) Sam, ya good-fo'-nuthin' fool, what ya wanna talk fo'?

MOTHER. Spoiled mah conjure, he did!

MAE. Sam, what ya sittin' dere fo'? Answer me, man! What ya wanna talk fo' an' spoil mamma's conjure? Ain't ya got sense enough to keep dat mouth o' yours shut while she's tryin' to get de spirits up?

MOTHER. Big black fool, dat's what he is!

MAE. Sam, what's de matter with ya? Sittin' dere with your eyes poppin' outa your head like a couple o' chicken eggs!

MOTHER. Crazy, dat's what he is!

MAE. Sam! Answer me! What's de matter with ya?

SAM (*hoarsely*). L-look!

MAE. Huh?

SAM. Standin' dere! In de corner!

(MOTHER *cries out, fading out quickly.*)

MAE (*up, in horror*). Dat man!

SAM. Yeah!

MAE. Who—who is he?

SAM. I—I dunno!

MAE. Mamma, look at dat man! Who is he, Mamma? (*In fright*) Mamma! Sam, look at her! Lyin' back in de chair!

SAM. Yeah!

MAE. Mouth hangin' open! Mamma! (*In wonder*) She—she passed out!

SAM. Look!

MAE. Huh?

SAM (*tensely*). Don' ya see him?

MAE. Wha' . . .

SAM. He's standin' right next to me. . . .

MAE. Who standin'? Who?

SAM. See'm?

MAE. Wha'— What're ya talkin' about?

SAM. Don' ya see'm? Standin' next to me?

MAE. Dey—dey ain't nobody dere!

SAM (*sharply*). What're ya talkin' about? Big man—bigger'n me!

MAE. Is ya crazy?

SAM (*sharply*). Is *you* crazy? Funny-lookin' man—big man —ain't white—ain't black!

MAE (*weepily*). Crazy in de head! (*Off*) Mamma! Wake up!

SAM. Ah tell ya he's standin' here! An' he's sayin' sumpin'! Lissen to him!

MAE. Nobody's sayin' nuthin'!

SAM. Lissen to him! Deh! Did ya hear him?

MAE (*weepily*). Nobody!

SAM (*sharply*). He's heah, Ah tell ya! An' he's sayin' sumpin' funny. Ah—Ah don' know what!

MAE (*weepily*). Oh, Mamma, Mamma! Wake up!

SAM. Yeah, Ah hear him clear now! He's sayin', "Genghis Khan"—"Genghis Khan." . . .

(*Musical transition.*)

(*Street sounds. One hears a street-corner orator speaking, back, but his words are unintelligible, continuing back behind.*)

FIRST MAN. And this, Mr. Harris, is Union Square.

HARRIS (*cultured voice—he is slumming*). Oh, yes, I've heard

84

of it. Where all the would-be world-savers get their chance, eh?

FIRST MAN. That's right! Chicago has its Bug-house Circle, London has its Hyde Park, but there's nothing like little old Union Square for crackpots!

HARRIS (*chuckling*). They don't even bother with soapboxes, do they?

FIRST MAN. Nope! Any spot'll do. They just begin talking away and pretty soon a crowd gathers and there they are!

HARRIS (*chuckling*). Don't even have to pay for a hall, is that it?

FIRST MAN. Right! Want to listen to a few?

HARRIS. Sure, why not?

FIRST MAN. Which one do you want to listen to? We've got parlor pinks, and religious crackpots, and world saviours and anything else you can think about.

HARRIS. That big buck Negro there—what's he talking about?

FIRST MAN. Let's push through the crowd and find out.

(*Fade-in* SAM's *following speech to give the impression that the men are moving toward him*.)

SAM (*he is speaking slowly, portentously, as if the words he is speaking are unfamiliar to him—as if he is being forced to say them*). And I say to all you who listen to me, join with me. For those who are not with me, are against me, and those shall I destroy! For that which I have set out to do, I will do! All the world shall be mine—from end to end, and all people shall bow before the might of Khan!

(*Crowd bursts into raucous cries, boos and cheers, continuing back behind.*)

HARRIS (*laughingly*). What in the world is he talking about?

FIRST MAN (*laughingly*). I haven't the slightest idea! Sounds as if he was recruiting men for a crusading army!

85

HARRIS. Listen to the crowd!

(*Crowd noise up for a few seconds, then down slightly behind.*)

HARRIS. Certainly having fun with the poor fellow!

(*Crowd noise back behind.*)

SAM (*in close, miserably*). But Ah tried, suh! Ah did jes' what ya told me to say in mah head! Ah tried to git 'em to join ya! Ah tried, Mister Genghis Khan. . . .

(*Musical transition.*)

CLANCY (*definite Irish accent*). Ah, I tell ye, Mac, bein' a desk sergeant ain't what it's cracked up to be! Here I sit, wearing out the seat of my pants, and I get about as much chance for gittin' any place as that inkwell there!

MAC. What's the beef, Sarg?

CLANCY. Opportunity, that's what it is!

MAC. Huh?

CLANCY. Don't you know nuthin'? Opportunity! I been readin' one of them books that tells ye how to get influence —you know. . . . It says ye got to grab hold of opportunity when it comes along. And I'm askin' ye, where's it to grab, me sittin' here spreadin' me rear!

MAC (*laughingly*). So you been readin' books, eh, Sarg?

CLANCY. Yeah, and don't think it don't make a fellow think, them books! It says there that a man should take a job where he gets chances—uh—comes in contact with opportunities, that's what it says! Now, I ask ye plain, Mac, what chances and what opportunity . . . ?

MAC. Hold it, Sarg! (*Chuckles*) Here comes opportunity!

CLANCY. Huh?

MAC. Colored boy . . . Looks as if he's gonna knock twice!

CLANCY. Aw!

86

SAM (*fade-in, hesitantly*). 'Scuse me, Mr. Policeman—suh— 'scuse me!

CLANCY (*in his professional attitude*). Well, what's on your mind?

SAM. 'Scuse me, suh. Sam's mah name—Big Sam Jones.

CLANCY. So what?

SAM. Ah—Ah want ya to lock me up, suh, please. . . .

CLANCY. Lock ye up? What're ye talkin' about?

SAM. Ya *gotta* lock me up, suh! If ya don't, Ah don't know what Ah'll do!

CLANCY. Say, who the devil are you?

SAM. Me, suh? Ah'm jest a house-painter. Sam Jones—Ah paints . . .

CLANCY. Who cares about that? What've you been up to?

SAM. Me, suh? Nuthin', suh! It's *him!*

CLANCY. Him?

SAM. Yes, suh, first he wants me to get 'im an army! Climbs right in mah head and says he wants an army! Lotta smart talk, too, that Ah don't understand jest yet, but dat Ah know—wants an army—big army—and me to go around and get it!

CLANCY. Mac, did you hear that?

MAC. The guy's nuts!

SAM. Oh, no, suh, no! Dat's true, Ah'm tellin' yuh! He's gotta lotta big ideas and wants me to go around talkin' to da people and get 'em in an army. He keeps on bangin' in my head to get 'im an army, but Ah'm jest Sam Jones . . . I dunno—if you'll help me, suh, maybe . . .

CLANCY (*interrupting*). Now wait a minute! Wait a minute! You keep talkin' like that and I'll be sendin' ye over to Bellevue to get your head looked into! Now, talk sense! What do ye want?

SAM. Well, suh, it's like this: Mae's ole lady, she conjured him up . . . An' ever since then . . .

(*Telephone rings sharply.*)

CLANCY (*sharply*). Hold it!

(*Telephone receiver off.*)

CLANCY. Sergeant Clancy, first district, speaking! (*Up, in excitement*) What! When! All right, sir! Right away!

(*Receiver up.*)

MAC. What is it, Sarg?

CLANCY. Plenty! Sixth Avenue subway! Fire!

(*Alarm bell ringing, back.*)

CLANCY (*up*). Every man out! Emergency call!

(*Murmur of policemen's voices coming in.*)

SAM. But, suh! How about me, suh? How about *me*?

CLANCY (*angrily*). Get away from me, will ye? Get out of here! Got more important things on my mind!

(*Murmur of men's voices ad libbing in excitement, "What is it, Sarg?" etc., continuing back behind.*)

SAM (*brokenly, in close*). Ah tried! Now Ah guess Ah *gotta* do what you want me to do, Mister Genghis Khan. . . .

(*Musical transition.*)

(*Board fade-in.*)

SAM. Ain't got nuthin', have ya? Want a job, don't ya! Yeah, a good job! Well, man, you listen to me, and you'll have somethin'! Pork chops in the belly and money in the pocket and a car in the garage! (*Fade*) You listen to me, man— you listen to me!

(DISCIPLE No. 1. *Through the above ad libs words of agreement such as: "That's all right! That's the truth! Yes, sir! I'm with you!" Continuing, off mike, saying it over and over until cue out.*)

SAM (*fade-in*). Now I'm talking to you, boy—I'm talking to

ya! Everybody shoves you around; well, you listen to me, you'll shove *them* around! Knock 'em down and kick 'em in the teeth! Everybody that laughed at you, you'll laugh at them! (*Fade*) You stick with me, boy, you stick with me!

(DISCIPLE No. 2. *Ad libs words of agreement through the above speech in same manner as* DISCIPLE No. 1 *did. At "Laughed at you" in above starts saying, "I'm with ya, Boss-man! I'm with ya, Boss-man!" over and over, off mike, continuing until cue.*)

SAM (*fade-in*). You'd better listen to me, man! You'd better listen to me! What you got to lose? You ain't got nuthin', so what you got to lose? Tired doin' the same things over and over every day, ain't ya? So listen to me! Join up with me and you'll have plenty fun! Everybody join up with me —black or white! Everybody'll have everything they want! I'm the Boss, so I'll make everything all right! Just listen to the Boss, and everything'll be all right! Do what the Boss says, and everything'll be all right! Trust in the Boss, and everything'll be all right! Believe in the Boss, and everything'll be all right!

(DISCIPLE No. 3 *ad libs words of agreement through above speech in the same manner as the other* DISCIPLE *did. At "I'm the Boss" in above starts saying, "I'm with you, Boss! I'm with you, Boss!" over and over, off mike, continuing until cue. For a few seconds we hear nothing but the worshipful cries of the* DISCIPLES *fade slowly.*)

(*Cross-fade piano playing in honky-tonk; murmur of customers in background.*)

VOICE No. 1 (*far back*). Couple of short ones, Joe!

VOICE No. 2 (*far back*). Comin' up!

VOICE No. 3 (*far back*). Whassa idea? I pay for that drink! See—I paid for that drink!

(*Ad libs back and continuing far, far behind.*)

SAM. So you fellas are with me?

(*The three* DISCIPLES *ad lib,* "Yes, Boss"—"Sure, Boss"— "We're with you, Boss.")

SAM. Then I'm satisfied! And the spirit in me is satisfied!

DISCIPLE NO. 1. What you mean the spirits in you, Boss?

SAM. Never you mind about the spirit in me, Fess. He climbed in me and he's in me deep, and now I know what I got to do!

DISCIPLE NO. 2 (*high-pitched voice*). What you got to do?

SAM. If you shut your mouth, I'll tell you. First, gotta organize.

(*The three* DISCIPLES *murmur,* "Yes, that's the truth, Boss." "That's right, Boss." "Sure, Boss.")

SAM. Get organized, that's it. And first I gotta organize you three! You, Sable!

DISCIPLE NO. 2. Yes, Boss?

SAM. You can read and write—well, I'm puttin' you in charge of the readin' and writin'! Goin' to print lots of stuff and tell everybody that the Boss is here!

DISCIPLE NO. 2. Sure, Boss, but what'll I write?

SAM. What I tell you! And I tell you to tell them anything! Just so they join the army! If they ain't got nothin', tell them they'll have somethin', and if they got somethin', tell them they'll keep that somethin' from those that ain't got nothin'! If they ain't got nothin' to do, tell them I'll *give* them somethin' to do! If they want marchin', tell them I'll *give* them marchin'! If they want fightin', tell them I'll *give* them fightin'! If they want to sit at home, tell them I'll let them *sit* at home! The Boss can do anythin'. Keep on writin', and if you keep on tellin' it to them even if they

don' listen to you at first, they'll listen to you at last! I'm
the Boss, and that's what I say!

DISCIPLE No. 2. Sure, Boss, sure!

SAM. Now it's your turn, Fess.

DISCIPLE No. 1. I'm listenin', Boss, I'm listenin'!

SAM. You'll be in charge of the money!

DISCIPLE No. 1. What money?

SAM. The money that you're goin' to be in charge of!

DISCIPLE No. 1. Where'm I goin' to get it?

SAM. Shut up and listen to the Boss!

DISCIPLE No. 1. Sure, Boss, sure!

SAM. Spirit in me says, you get the money from those that
got somethin' who think that by givin' me the money they'll
keep those that got nothin' from gettin' their hands on their
somethin'! And those that got nothin', they'll get money
some place to give you, so that they'll be in on the somethin' when the great day comes!

DISCIPLE No. 1. Ain't that the truth!

SAM. Sure, it's the truth! Now you, Mistuh Roarin'.

DISCIPLE No. 3 (*he has a deep voice*). I'm with you, Boss.

SAM. And you, Roarin', you goin' to be in charge of the
kickin' around and shovin' around and gettin' my army
together that'll cover the world! There'll be those that'll
stand in our way who don' know about the spirit in me,
and you gotta get the young ones and strong ones to stand
around and help me shove my way up to the top!

DISCIPLE No. 3. I'll do it, Boss! I'll do it!

SAM. Sure, you'll do it! I'm the Boss, and I say you'll do it!

DISCIPLE No. 3. That's the truth! That's the truth!

SAM. It's the truth of the spirit in me! Tell them what they
want to believe is the truth, get them hatin', get them
fightin', and shove right up to the top!

THE THREE DISCIPLES (*in unison*). Hail to the Boss! Hail to the Boss! Hail to the Boss!

BARTENDER (*fade-in angrily*). Hey, you guys! Stop that yellin'!

DISCIPLE No. 2. Once more, boys!

THE THREE DISCIPLES (*in unison*). Hail to the Boss! Hail to the Boss! Hail to the Boss!

BARTENDER. I tell you, shut up! What kinda place you think I'm runnin' here? Now get outa here, you loud-mouthed bums!

DISCIPLE No. 1. Hey, who you think you're talkin' to? This is the Boss and we're the Junior Bosses!

DISCIPLE No. 2. That's right, and we're takin' over!

BARTENDER. Wha-at?

SAM. That's right, we're takin' over!

BARTENDER. Why, you . . .

SAM. Shut up! Brother Roarin'—as head of the pushin' and shovin' around—smack this guy down!

DISCIPLE No. 3. It's a pleasure!

(*Smack of fist.*)

VOICE (*far back*). Fight!

BARTENDER. Why, you—why, you . . .

SAM. Smack him again!

DISCIPLE No. 2. Knock him down!

(*Ad lib of voices far back: "Fight him!" "Hit him!" "Let me in on it!" etc.*)

DISCIPLE No. 1. Look out for that bottle, Boss!

SAM. Don't hit me! Don't hit me!

DISCIPLE No. 2. Hide under the table, Boss!

(*Bring up sounds of battle with piano crashing, etc., fade-out slowly.*)

(*Board fade.* JUDGE *banging gavel, murmur of courtroom.*)

JUDGE. Order in the court! Order in the court!

(*Murmur dies out.*)

JUDGE. If I've any more disturbances, I'll clear the court! Where were we? Oh, yes, the apparent facts are that you four men went into this beer cellar and created a public disturbance! Before I pass sentence, have any of you anything further to say for yourselves?

SAM. I'se got plenty to say!

JUDGE. Oh, have you? How did you hurt that arm?

SAM. Defendin' the truth!

JUDGE. The truth?

POLICEMAN (*back*). That's what *he* says!

JUDGE. What's that, officer?

POLICEMAN (*fade-in a bit*). Your Honor, he hit his arm falling under the table to get out of the way of the beer bottles!

JUDGE (*amused*). Really! Well, er—whatever your name is—Sam Jones—what more have you to say for yourself?

SAM. The highest shall be the lowest, and when the great day comes, I shall come climbin' over the lowest and reach the highest!

JUDGE. Wha-at?

SAM. My followers will tell you! (*Up*) Who's to blame for our misery?

THE THREE DISCIPLES (*in unison*). The system!

SAM. Who's behind the system?

THE THREE DISCIPLES (*in unison*). Everybody—we—don't—like!

SAM. What am I to you?

THE THREE DISCIPLES (*in unison*). Our faith!

SAM. What else?

THE THREE DISCIPLES (*in unison*). Our hope!

SAM. What else?

THE THREE DISCIPLES (*in unison*). Our boss! Hail to the Boss! Hail to the Boss! Hail to the Boss!

(*Pandemonium in courtroom, banging of gavel.*)

JUDGE. Order in the court! Order in the court! The bailiff will clear the court!

VOICE (*back*). Clear the court! Clear the court!

(*We hear the courtroom being cleared, murmur of voices fading, banging of gavel.*)

JUDGE. Quiet! Quiet! Now, then, Boss, or whatever your name is, I should send you to have your head examined, but I don't think that would do much good! I'm sentencing your loud-mouthed Disciples to thirty days each in the county jail and—you know what I'm going to do for you?—I'm going to give you sixty days. Now, what do you say to that?

SAM. The spirit in me says that's okay.

JUDGE. Wha-at?

SAM. The spirit says, now I'll have time to write the truth of how I and all who believe in me will conquer the world! The truth about everybody I hate, and what I'm goin' to do to them and how I'm goin' to do it! Yeah, now I'll have time to write a book, and I'll call it *My Glory!*

(JUDGE *breaks into guffaw of laughter, continuing. Other people in the courtroom join in. Music takes up the laughing strain as transition. Bring in great chorus of laughter down on cue and continuing behind.*)

VOICE NO. 1 (*back, shouting*). Did you read about him?

(*Laughter up as transition, then continuing down behind.*)

VOICE NO. 2. He calls himself the Boss!

(*Laughter up, then down behind.*)

VOICE NO. 3. Can you imagine—writing a book in jail!

(*Laughter up, then down behind.*)

VOICE. Just a crackpot! Who'll ever listen to him?

(*Laughter up—board fade slowly—cut—open fast.*)

(*Wind, down, and continuing intermittently behind.*)

DISCIPLE No. 2. (*This entire scene should be played quietly, in close, in a conspiratorial manner*). We've been waitin' for you a long time, Boss.

DISCIPLE No. 3. Yeah, that extra thirty days . . .

DISCIPLE No. 2. Long time!

DISCIPLE No. 1. Ain't it the truth!

SAM (*with quiet dignity*). It's all right, boys, I'm here now. For sixty days the spirit in me has been writin' and thinkin'. I know just what I got to do. Are you with me?

DISCIPLE No. 2. Sure, Boss!

DISCIPLE No. 3. All the way!

DISCIPLE No. 1. Just what you say!

SAM. They laughed at us. Laughed all over at me. The spirit in me don't like that laughin'! No, suh! Well, the laughin's goin' to stop. I'm goin' to clear the streets for my battalions! The great day's dawnin'!

THE THREE DISCIPLES (*murmuring in unison*). Great day's dawnin'!

SAM. Down with the system!

THE THREE DISCIPLES (*murmuring in unison*). Down with the system!

SAM. Somethin's gonna happen.

THE THREE DISCIPLES (*murmuring in unison*). Somethin's gonna happen. . . .

SAM. Wake up the city!

THE THREE DISCIPLES. Wake up de city!

SAM. Now, listen—round the corner is de armory. Guns dere —an' bullets that make 'em stop the laughin'. Make 'em lissen to me . . . (*In close, slowly*) Armory round the corner . . .

(*Musical transition.*)

(*Board fade-in of sound of busy street in center of town, back behind and fading in together with:*)

NEWSBOY (*Italian*). Paper! Read all about it! Get your evenin' paper! Don't go home without your evenin' paper! Read all about it! They're all dead!

ALDERMAN (*fade-in fast, interrupting laughingly*). Now, just a minute there, Rico, just a minute!

NEWSBOY. Hiya, Mr. Alderman, you want a paper, eh?

ALDERMAN (*laughing*). I certainly do, but what's this about "they're all dead"?

NEWSBOY. Aw, nobody buy a paper, I get mad, so I say, "They're all dead!" you know—just a joke!

ALDERMAN. Now that's a fine thing, standing in front of the city hall and yelling "They're all dead!" What kind of reputation you going to give this town?

NEWSBOY. Aw, I didn't mean it; it's just a joke.

ALDERMAN. All right, Rico, I'm joking too! Give me one of each.

NEWSBOY. Sure, Mr. Alderman, sure! Here you are!

ALDERMAN. And here *you* are!

NEWSBOY. Say! Thanks very much! Sonamagum, I vote for you next time! Betcha life!

ALDERMAN. Well, I should hope so! And you tell your friends — (*Stops suddenly*) Say!

NEWSBOY. Whassamatter, Mr. Alderman?

ALDERMAN. Am I seeing things?

NEWSBOY. Huh?

ALDERMAN. On the cupola!

NEWSBOY. Huh?

ALDERMAN. Top of the city hall! Am I seeing things, or . . . ?

NEWSBOY. Holy cats! It's a guy!

ALDERMAN. He'll fall! Police! Police!

(*Bring in crowd—ad libs such as:*)

VOICES. Man upon the top of the city hall!
   Must be crazy!
   Fall and break his neck!
   Who is he?

(*Bring crowd noise up: police whistles, sirens, etc., fade far back.*)

(*Sound of men running up flight of stairs behind.*)

OFFICER No. 1 (*breathlessly*). Yeah—right at the top of the stairs?

OFFICER No. 2. Ya sure it leads out there?

OFFICER No. 1. I'm tellin' ya! Winda there—you can climb right out . . .

OFFICER No. 2. Not me—*you!* Coupla hundred feet to the street! I ain't . . .

OFFICER No. 1. All right, all right, we'll just yell at him! Wait 'til the fire wagons get here. They can . . .

(*Crowd roar very faintly back behind.*)

OFFICER No. 1. Will ya listen to the crowd down there!

OFFICER No. 2. Hope he don't jump. Chief'll kick us around for . . .

(*Stair sounds out.*)

OFFICER No. 1. Hold it! Now careful—don't let him see us at first, or he might jump!

OFFICER No. 2. I don't see 'em!

OFFICER No. 1. Other side of the dome!

OFFICER No. 2. Climb out!

OFFICER No. 1. Ya think I'm a boid? (*Calling*) Hey, you out there!

SAM (*back*). What you want?

OFFICER No. 1. Police officers! Come on off that dome! You're breakin' the law!

SAM (*back*). *I* am de law!

OFFICER No. 1. Did you hear that, Max? He . . .

OFFICER No. 2. There he comes! Come on, boy, right this way! We . . .

OFFICER No. 1 (*up*). Look out! Tommy-gun! He's got . . .

(*Roar of Thompson sub-machine gun back; men cry out; fade-in machine-gun shots full, out cold on cue.*)

SAM (*in satisfaction*). That does it! Great day now! Can't let nobody talk to me—got to talk to *dem!* (*Up full*) You down dere! Lissen to me! De Boss talkin'! All you people down dere! Lissen to de Boss! I'm talkin' to you to tell you I'm takin' over! Ain't got no time for fancy stuff! De spirit in me says, now is de time! All of you down there, my army and me just takin' over! Me on top and you down there—me tellin' you what to do and you doin' it, and you don't have to think no more, 'cause I'll do all the thinkin' for you! Now, ain't dat wonderful? No more thinkin'! Gonna give you marchin'! Gonna give ya bands playin'! Gonna give ya fancy uniforms! Yes, suh—uniforms for everybody—men and the women-folk—and even the little children! Oh, most of all the children! Spirit in me says, most of all the children! Start the children on the right path to glory and everythin's just kopisetik! Lissen to me, you down there—all of you with your faces turned up lookin' at me! It's *me,* the *Boss,* talkin' to you! No more thinkin'— bands a-playin'—kick around the people that we don' like— lock and string up anybody don't do just like they're told— anybody don't hail the Boss! 'Cause the Boss, he's your best friend! Yes, suh! Boss, he's gonna make you greatest people in the world! Yes, suh! There'll be shootin', and there'll be fightin', and there'll be dyin'; but you'll be the greatest people in the world! I'll make you that! *Me! Me! Me!* And (*Fade fast*) nobody'll have to think no more! Nobody! Nobody think! Just fight and die for the glory of the Boss! Now I want ya to listen to me close! Everyone of ya! Every man and woman and de children—lissen close! Ah'm gonna tell ya more—keep nothin' from ya! Boss won't keep nothin' from ya! Boss, he's your friend, your pal, your leader! Lissen to the word of your big Boss! Lissen to him, all of ya! I'm talkin' to ya! (*Etc. ad lib far back to give picture of our having gone down to crowd far below, leaving him exhorting from high above.*)

(*On cue with above fade, slowly bring in crowd in street below. At first we hear general murmur, then, as we get closer, murmur turns into excited specific ad libs such as "Killed two cops!" "What's he sayin'?" etc. ad lib, down on cue far behind.*)

DETECTIVE. But, chief . . .

CHIEF. No, no, not going to risk any more lives! If he turns that gun on the crowd down here . . .

DETECTIVE. Well, should we . . . ?

CHIEF. Yes, yes, right away!

DETECTIVE. Okay, chief! (*Up*) Sergeant!

VOICE. Yes, sir?

DETECTIVE. Get him from here?

VOICE. Yes, sir.

DETECTIVE. Okay. Pick him off.

VOICE. Right!

(*Rifle shot in close.*)

(*Concerted gasp of crowd, followed by roar, down behind.*)

DETECTIVE. You hit him!

99

VOICE. He didn't fall!

CHIEF. Up there! Get him, men!

(*Fade crowd quickly and hold far, far behind:*)

SAM (*dying, gasping for breath*). I—I—I tried to do—just what ya told me to do, Mistuh Genghis Khan. . . . (*Breath out in death.*)

(*Musical transition.*)

(*Rattle of newspaper behind.*)

AVERAGE MAN. Hey, Mary, did you read in the paper about that fellow up on top of the City Hall last night? Crazy, eh? But, you know, while I was reading about it, I couldn't help but think, what if someone with ideas like that—or, you know, like the fool said—with the *spirit* in him like that—really got into power somewhere! (*Pause, then chuckles*) Ah, what's the matter with me? It couldn't really happen!

(*Musical curtain.*)

THE WORD

After a while, you begin to look for escape. You reason, you rationalize, but it's too much. So you go to the bottom of a bottle, or to a woman, or whatever your most potent release is, to get away from the pound of those headlines, the radio, and your own inner consciousness of what's taking place.

And, if you are a writer, you write something like The Word.

THE WORD

ANNOUNCER. A boy and a girl are honeymooning in New York. They have just arrived in the city. This is a day of great new excitements for them. . . .
(*Sound of busy street, newsboys, etc., and continuing behind.*)
EVE. Michael! Not really!
MICHAEL. It's the truth!
EVE. But that's so much money, Michael!
MICHAEL (*reproving laughingly*). Darling! Don't you know it's bad manners for the bride to talk about money the *first* day of the honeymoon?
EVE. But a dollar and ten cents just to go to the top of a building!
MICHAEL. But we'll be able to see the whole city from up there!
EVE. There's so much to see down *here!*
MICHAEL. Now, Eve, there were two things I promised myself on my first honeymoon, and one of them was not to count the pennies for once in my life, and the other was to see New York from the top of Radio City. All right, here we are and up we go! (*Fade*) Come on!
(*Up with street sounds, then down behind.*)
VOICE. Express to the observation roof! Going up!
MICHAEL. In here, Eve.
EVE. Yes.
ELEVATOR MAN. Face front, please.
(*All street sounds out with sound of closing elevator door.*

Rush of air as express elevator rises, continuing back be-hind.)

MICHAEL (*down*). Eve!

EVE. Hm?

MICHAEL. Forget all about what's happening outside—news-papers—and things. . . . Don't let it spoil—*this!*

EVE (*simply*). Nothing can spoil being with you, Michael.

MICHAEL. Sweet. . . .

EVE. Can't hardly feel the elevator moving! It is moving, Michael?

MICHAEL. Aw, sure! Look at the lights. Twenty-fifth floor al-ready.

EVE. Doesn't seem possible! Ooh—my ears!

MICHAEL. Mine too!

EVE. Because we're going so fast?

MICHAEL. No, something about air pressure . . . You know, like getting on top of a mountain. Gee, look at those lights. We're at the fiftieth floor—at least *they* say so!

EVE. It's so scary—and—and wonderful!

MICHAEL. Just think—a hundred and two floors up in the air!

ELEVATOR MAN (*off slightly*). Not on *this* elevator, mister.

MICHAEL. Eh?

ELEVATOR MAN. You have to change at the eightieth and then at the eighty-sixth again.

MICHAEL. Oh! Oh, thanks! (*Sotto*) Look, Eve! Seventieth floor already!

EVE. I'll bet they're fooling us!

MICHAEL. Yeah.

ELEVATOR MAN (*off slightly*). I heard there's an extra paper out that the war's gonna . . .

MICHAEL. Please!

ELEVATOR MAN. Huh?

MICHAEL. If you don't mind, we don't want to talk about those things.

ELEVATOR MAN. Oh—yeah. . . . I don't blame ya. . . .

(*Elevator whine diminishing as elevator comes to a stop.*)

ELEVATOR MAN. Far as we go.

(*Sound of elevator door opening.*)

MICHAEL. Where do we . . . ?

ELEVATOR MAN. Next elevator, right over there, sir.

MICHAEL. Thanks. (*Down*) Better hold on to my arm, Eve.

EVE. Yes. . . . Why does everyone have to talk about war all the time, Michael?

MICHAEL. That's just the way it is, I guess. . . .

ELEVATOR MAN (*off slightly*). Going up.

MICHAEL. Come ahead, Eve.

ELEVATOR MAN (*in*). Watch your step, please.

(*Sound of elevator door closing. Whine of express elevator continuing back behind.*)

MICHAEL (*sotto*). I wonder how much you can see up there.

EVE. All New York, the guide book says. . . .

ELEVATOR MAN (*off slightly*). Observation roof next stop. One hundred and second floor.

MICHAEL (*sotto*). And I used to think that I was getting up high when I climbed the apple tree.

(EVE *giggles.*)

(*Elevator whine out behind.*)

ELEVATOR MAN. Observation roof—hundred and second floor.

(*Sound: Elevator door opening.*)

MICHAEL. Gosh! Express is right! All right, Eve. This is it!

EVE. Will the wind blow—will it . . . ? Why, Michael, it's all glassed in!

MICHAEL. Yes!

EVE. Oh, Michael! How wonderful!

MICHAEL. Gosh!

EVE (*fading*). Michael, come over here!

MICHAEL. Huh?

EVE (*fade-in*). Look—the ocean out there!

MICHAEL. I can see the Statue of Liberty!

EVE. Oh, it's wonderful!

MICHAEL. And you didn't want to come up here!

EVE. Like the world—right under us!

MICHAEL. Not scared a bit, are you?

Eve. Why should I be? It's just wonderful! (*Fade*) Look—over here!

MICHAEL (*laughingly*). Will you quit running around here like a doodlebug? What . . . ?

EVE (*in full*). The bridges over the river! Which one's that?

MICHAEL. I dunno—Brooklyn or something!

EVE. So many buildings! I—I had no idea New York was so—so spread out! (*Fade*) So many buildings! So wonderful!

MICHAEL. Yeah! From up here!

EVE (*fade back in*). What? What did you say, Michael?

MICHAEL. I said it's all wonderful—from up here! But get down there and—well, I bet it's like one of those Hollywood—you know—glamour stars when she gets up in the morning!

EVE (*laughing softly*). Michael, what do you know about things like that?

MICHAEL. I know you're super-colossal or something when *you* wake up!

EVE. Oh!

MICHAEL. You are! Your eyelashes sort of flutter, and then you stretch just like a little pup dog. . . .

EVE. Like a pup dog! Oh, Michael, is that romantic?

MICHAEL. Oh, I don't know the words. I just know that I'm gladder every minute that you married me.

EVE. *You* married *me*.

MICHAEL. Don't argue with your husband.

EVE (*in close*). Husband . . .

MICHAEL (*in close*). Eve. . . . Lips are so soft . . .

EVE. Yours aren't. . . .

MICHAEL. Glad no one else is up here.

EVE (*shoving him away laughingly*). All right, Michael! Two dollars and twenty cents to make love to me or to see the sights?

MICHAEL (*chuckling*). I married a beautiful cash register.

EVE. Listen, Mr. Smith, will you let go of me?

MICHAEL. Aw!

EVE. You're going to see me for ninety-nine years, and maybe this is the last time we'll be able to get away and see New York this way and (*In surprise*) Michael!

MICHAEL. Wha . . .

EVE. Look over there!

MICHAEL. How do you like that! Clouds!

EVE. Where did they come from?

MICHAEL. The usual place clouds come from, I suppose.

EVE. But so quickly.

MICHAEL. We're up plenty high!

EVE. Look at them—coming right at us!

MICHAEL. Strong wind, I guess!

EVE. Michael, this is so exciting. Up in the clouds!

MICHAEL. Made to order for you and me!

(*Distant rumble of thunder.*)

MICHAEL. Oh, oh! Rain!

EVE. There goes the rest of our day!

MICHAEL. Sure is a good thing they've got this place glassed in!

EVE (*cries out*). Oh!

MICHAEL. Eve! Only lightning.

(*Crash of thunder in closer.*)

EVE. Oh, no!

MICHAEL. Eve! You've been in thunderstorms before!

EVE. Michael!

MICHAEL. Eve! What is it?

EVE (*awe in voice*). The clouds! They're fighting!

MICHAEL. Huh?

EVE. Look at them—fighting each other!

MICHAEL. Is that any reason to be afraid? Gosh! Thunder clouds always sort of boil around!

(*Thunder crash.*)

EVE (*slowly*). Like armies—fighting!

MICHAEL (*in wonder*). Eve, what kind of talk is that?

(*Thunder crash again.*)

EVE. Armies—fighting . . .

MICHAEL. Why do you keep saying that?

EVE. I can't help it. I keep thinking . . .

MICHAEL. Well, *don't* think! Remember, we said—our honey-moon—we wouldn't think about anything but—but *us!*

EVE. This *is* us! How can I be happy when all over the world . . . ?

(*Crash of thunder again.*)

MICHAEL. All right. I *will* talk about it. . . . I'll talk about it once and for all, then you and I won't have to talk about it any more! Gosh, I don't know anything about—about those things the newspapers are always talking about! Maybe I'm not so smart as the people who live in this town and all the other big towns, when it comes to dodging taxicabs and throwin' wisecracks, but I know this: I don't want to own everything I can get my hands on, and I know that it isn't right for some people to have too much when some people have too little, and I know if I have to fight I will fight, but, if I fight, it'll be for what *I* know is right, for the kind of world where all the little people have a chance, no matter what they look like or what their name is or what their blood is; because I know that no matter what any little dictator says, people all over the world are just like you and me! All *they* want and all *I* want is happy work and someone they care for to work for, and a little time left over in which just to enjoy being alive!

(*Thunder crash.*)

EVE. I love you, Michael. . . .

MICHAEL. Let's go down. . . .

EVE. No—just a moment more!

(*Thunder—back.*)

EVE. Storm's breaking . . .

MICHAEL. Yes, I guess it is. Gosh! First time in my life I ever talked like that!

EVE. You're very good, Michael.

MICHAEL. Not bright—but good.

(*Thunder far, far back.*)

EVE. Michael, look!

MICHAEL. Look at what?

EVE. Just can't see anything down there.

MICHAEL. Yeah! Air's full of mist, that's why.

EVE. See things—and yet you don't see them.

MICHAEL. Let's go, huh?

EVE. All right.

MICHAEL. Hold on to my arm. If it's still raining when we get down, we'll take a taxi back to the hotel.

Eve. All right.

Michael. I guess this is the button I press to get the elevator up here. (*As he presses*) Mm! Well, that ought to bring them up. Gosh, thunderstorms and everything. . . .

Eve. It's been quite an experience, hasn't it?

Michael. Yeah! I sure jumped out of my skin when you screamed. I mean when you saw those thunder clouds.

Eve. I didn't scream, Michael!

Michael. Well, you certainly did—kind of. (*Chuckling*) I sure don't know much about women, I guess. I mean you were afraid of the clouds, and then you weren't afraid of the thunder and lightning!

Eve. Clouds—were—horrible.

Michael (*laughing disparagingly*). Aw! Hey, what's the matter with that elevator?

Eve. Ring again.

Michael. That's all I've been doing!

Eve. Something must be wrong with it. The button . . .

Michael. Yeah! No answer—that's plain enough!

Eve. Don't be so impatient!

Michael. Well, we certainly can't *walk* down!

Eve. They'll come up for us.

Michael. Gosh, my thumb's getting sore punching this thing. Something sure is out of order!

Eve. Maybe we *had* better walk down.

Michael. A hundred and two floors!

Eve. No, I mean just to the next landing where we can get the next elevator! See—stairway!

Michael. Okay. I guess there's nothing else to do about it! Come on!

(*Footsteps.*)

Eve. Don't walk so fast, dear!

MICHAEL. What a life!

EVE. Oh, it isn't so bad walking *down*stairs.

MICHAEL (*chuckles*). You're swell! Here—take my arm! Down we go, Mrs. Smith. Elevators are all right, but me, I'll take the old-fashioned horse!

EVE (*fondly*). Crazy!

(*Musical transition.*)

(*Sound of walking downstairs continuing behind.*)

MICHAEL. Step a hundred and fifty—fifty-one—fifty-two— fifty . . .

EVE. Michael! Look! That door says eighty-six!

MICHAEL. Hallelujah, we're here!

(*Going downstairs out. Sound of opening heavy door behind.*)

MICHAEL (*with effort*). Sure a heavy door! All right, Eve, go through.

EVE. Yes. . . .

MICHAEL. There! Now we'll find out what was the matter! Elevators—yeah, there they are.

(*Two people walking across floor.*)

EVE. Doors are open.

MICHAEL. Yeah!

(*Footsteps out.*)

MICHAEL. Gosh! Where are the elevator men?

EVE. Maybe we just better wait.

MICHAEL. Wait! I want to ride! Where are they?

EVE. Nobody in the hall.

MICHAEL (*calls—slight echo*). Hey!

EVE (*aghast*). Michael, don't!

MICHAEL. Gotta get someone to run the contraptions! (*Up*) Hey! Elevator man!

EVE. They won't like it. . . .

MICHAEL. Well, gosh, *I* don't like being stuck up here! (*Up echo*) Hey, is there someone here to run these elevators?

EVE (*after pause*). No one . . .

MICHAEL. Now what'll we do?

EVE. The last elevator stopped at the eightieth floor, didn't it?

MICHAEL. You mean walk again?

EVE. Guess we have to.

MICHAEL. Yeah. Now, what could have happened to 'em? (*Musical transition.*)

MICHAEL (*fade-in, board—calling—slight echo*). Hey! Hey, isn't there anyone here? Hey, we want to get downstairs! Hey!

EVE. It's no use, dear.

MICHAEL. There's got to be somebody on *this* floor!

EVE. Don't get so excited, Michael!

MICHAEL. Well, gosh, eighty floors . . . We can't walk all *that* way!

EVE. We'll *have* to!

MICHAEL. Telephone!

EVE. Hmmmmm?

MICHAEL. Yeah, telephone—that's it! I'll call the operator and tell her what's happened! (*Fade*) Come on!

EVE. Mike, wait for me!

(*Door opening off slightly.*)

EVE. Michael, you can't go in there.

MICHAEL. Come on!

EVE. It's a private office.

MICHAEL. Sure, but they won't mind if I . . . Say! Can you beat that!

EVE. No one here. . . .

MICHAEL. Gone off with the elevator men, I'll bet you! Well, at least they left the telephone!

(*Telephone receiver off hook.*)

MICHAEL. Hope I can dial this thing right. . . . Yeah, here it says "operator."

(*Dialing once.*)

EVE. Michael, they won't like it at all if they come back in here and find we've walked right in without . . .

MICHAEL. Gosh!

EVE. What's the matter?

MICHAEL. The telephone! Here—listen!

EVE. Sounds—sort of dead.

MICHAEL. I'll say! Here—give it to me! Got to get *somebody!*

(*Clicking of telephone behind.*)

MICHAEL. Hey! Hey, listen, operator! How about answering? Operator! Operator!

EVE. It's no use, Michael.

(*Clicking out with:*)

MICHAEL. Yeah. . . . (*Laughs shortly*) Huh? Is this a mess!

EVE. Have to walk down—I guess.

MICHAEL. Where *is* everyone in this building? Gosh, you'd think . . .

EVE. Michael! Maybe there's been a fire!

MICHAEL. Fire? Yeah, maybe . . .

EVE. Michael, quick! Let's get to the stairway and get out of here! Quick, Michael!

(*Musical transition. Music down and continuing behind.*)

(*Two hurrying downstairs.*)

EVE (*breathlessly*). How far have we gone?

MICHAEL. Five or six floors, I guess. Hold tight to my arm!

(*Music up as transition, and then down again behind:*)

(*Steps—a little slower than before.*)

EVE. The whole building can't be empty, Michael!

MICHAEL. I tried every office on that floor, I tell you! There was no one! No one!

(*Music up as transition, then down and continuing behind.*)

(*Footsteps very slow now, as if they were very tired.*)

EVE. It can't be a fire, Michael.

MICHAEL. No—no smoke or anything.

EVE. But where *is everyone?* Michael, *where?*

(*Music up as transition . . . then segue into very weary footsteps continued behind.*)

EVE. But, Michael . . .

MICHAEL. Honey—I'm as tired trying to figure it out as I am walking down the whole blasted hundred and two floors. Floor after floor . . . Offices all fixed up as if people were working in them and no one there! I—I give up, I tell you!

EVE (*sharply*). Michael!

MICHAEL. Huh!

EVE. The war!

MICHAEL. Huh?

EVE. I mean the war news—everyone ran out into the street!

MICHAEL. Now, Eve, does that make sense? A whole skyscraper emptied out just to grab newspapers?

EVE. Michael . . .

MICHAEL (*going right on*). About a war that's all the way over the ocean? Aw, that makes about as little sense as everything else!

(*Footsteps out with:*)

MICHAEL (*sighs*). Well, this is it!

EVE. Are we . . . ?

MICHAEL. So help me! Main floor—all out . . . Gosh, my legs!

EVE. Michael, don't sit down! Hurry!

MICHAEL. Hurry! Where?

EVE. Out of here—the street—don't you want to know what's happened?

MICHAEL. Well—well, yeah, sure! Oh, that door says to the street! (*Fades*) Let's go!

EVE. Wait for me, Michael!

MICHAEL. Sure glad to get out of this place! Come on—out we go!

EVE. Yes!

(*Sound of street entrance-door opening, followed by soft wail of wind which continues intermittently behind.*)

EVE (*in great surprise*). Michael!

MICHAEL. Gosh!

EVE (*tears in voice*). Oh, Michael!

MICHAEL (*his voice belies his words*). It's all right, dear. It's all right.

EVE. Michael, what's happened?

(*Wind sighs.*)

MICHAEL (*dazedly*). Not a person on the streets . . .

EVE. There were so many!

MICHAEL. Yeah!

EVE. Michael! Michael! Listen!

MICHAEL (*after pause*). I don't hear anything!

(*Wind sighs softly.*)

EVE. Listen!

MICHAEL. Wind!

EVE. That's it! That's it! Only the wind! Michael, don't you remember? Ever since we got to New York—all day yesterday—all night—morning—the noise, Michael . . . Don't you remember the noise?

MICHAEL (*breathes the word*). Yes, I . . .

EVE. And now nothing but the wind! (*Building*) What's

happened? Why is it so quiet now? Where are the people? (*Up, almost hysterically*) *Michael, tell me!*

(*Musical transition.*)

(*Sound of footsteps of two people walking slowly along street behind.*)

MICHAEL (*down wearily*). Do you want to rest?

EVE. No! Just keep walking.

MICHAEL. All right. . . .

EVE. If we'd only meet—*one!* Michael, if we'd meet one person, someone—anyone . . .

MICHAEL (*breaking out*). Eve, stop it! Of course we'll meet someone! We've *got* to! There's millions of people in this town! Millions, I tell you!

EVE. Not a living thing—horse—dog—nothing. . . .

MICHAEL (*sharply*). There's an explanation, I tell you! There's an explanation for everything! Everyone's gone somewhere, that's all. Gone somewhere!

EVE (*after pause, slowly*). Where have they gone, Michael?

(*Wind sighs.*)

MICHAEL (*sharply*). Careful! Automobile!

EVE. It's standing still, like all the rest . . .

MICHAEL. Crazy people! Leave their car standing right in the middle of the street. They'll come back. They've got to! Millions of people, I tell you! (*Up, shouting*) People! Where are you? People! Hey! Somebody! Come out! Blast you! Come out! People! (*Etc., ad lib.*)

EVE (*pleadingly, in close, on cue through above speech*). No, no, please, Michael. Stop! You're frightening me! Empty streets! Stop yelling to them, Michael! (*Up, almost screamingly*) Michael, sto-o-op!

(MICHAEL *stops with above cry.*)

EVE (*weepily*). Stop! (*Weeps.*)

MICHAEL (*he too begins to cry*). Oh, Eve!

EVE. Hold me.

MICHAEL. What's happened to us? *What!* (*Recovering self slowly*) No—got to stop asking questions! Got to keep going . . . Got to find someone . . . They'll tell us. They'll . . . (*In surprise*) Eve! What—what is it, Eve?

EVE. Michael, I just thought!

MICHAEL. Thought *what?*

EVE. All these empty streets . . . Michael, listen to me! What if there *is* no one else?

MICHAEL. Huh?

EVE. What if you and I—are the only ones left?

(*Musical transition.*)

(*Wind sighs.*)

EVE (*very weary*). Michael . . .

MICHAEL. Yes. . . .

EVE. I—I can't walk another step.

MICHAEL. All right, we'll rest.

EVE. Where?

MICHAEL. Anywhere . . . Doesn't matter much, does it? (*Laughs shortly*) All New York's ours! You ought to know that by now. (*Laughs without mirth.*)

EVE. No, no, don't.

MICHAEL. Look! You know where we are?

EVE. No. . . .

MICHAEL. Broadway! Times Square! Well, I give you Times Square! It's all yours! Wedding present!

EVE. Michael, I'm so tired.

MICHAEL (*going right on*). Yeah, yours! (EVE *tries to interrupt*) Shops and big signs and all the taxicabs and busses and cars standing around! Yours, Eve! Yours to have or to lose or burn up or . . .

Eve (*sharply*). Michael, please!

MICHAEL. I—I'm sorry, honey. Guess I'm a little goofy! Let's keep goin', huh?

Eve. All right. . . .

(MICHAEL *sighs*.)

Eve. Tired?

MICHAEL. Yeah. . . .

Eve. It's going to get dark soon.

MICHAEL. Yeah. . . .

Eve (*hesitantly*). Will there—be light?

MICHAEL. No.

Eve. How do you know?

MICHAEL. I tried the light switches all along the way.

Eve (*slowly*). I won't be afraid of the dark.

MICHAEL. Guess that's one advantage we've got, coming from the country.

Eve. There'll be—people there, won't there?

MICHAEL (*slowly*). I don't think so.

Eve. Why do you say that?

MICHAEL. When we went into that store before—there were radio sets—*battery ones*. I tried them when you weren't looking. There was nothing on the air.

Eve. What does that mean?

MICHAEL. It means—what you said before—maybe it's true.

Eve. We're the only—the only . . .

MICHAEL. Yeah!

Eve (*sighs*). Somehow, I'm not as frightened as I was. . . .

MICHAEL. Me neither. My head . . . I'm just all mixed up, that's all. They left the doors open and the automobiles right in the middle of the street and—and everything's just as if they stopped right in the middle of what they were doing! But *why—why?* That word's got me dizzy—chasing around in my head!

Eve (*dawning wonder in her voice*). Michael!

Michael. Millions of people—where have they disappeared to? If we only had some idea—any idea?

Eve (*repeats*). Michael!

Michael. What's the matter? Why are you . . . ?

Eve. That newspaper! Right at your feet!

Michael. Huh?

Eve. Pick it up! The headlines!

(*Paper rattle.*)

Michael (*reads*). "War fury rages. Armies march in Europe." Well?

Eve. The headline . . .

Michael. What of it? The same one as this morning!

Eve. Couldn't *that* be the answer?

Michael. Answer to what? What are you talking about?

Eve. Why, they—*disappeared?*

Michael. Eve, get hold of yourself! What's a war thousands of miles away got to do with *this?*

Eve. Maybe—it's the same over there.

Michael (*sharply*). People gone?

Eve. Yes!

Michael (*sharply*). Let's keep goin'! No! The curb—let's sit here.

(*Wind sighs.*)

Eve. All right.

Michael. Now, you've got to tell me what you started to say. . . .

Eve. Don't laugh at me when I say it, Michael.

Michael. Just tell me!

EVE. The war—people killing each other—maybe God got tired of it.

MICHAEL (*blankly*). *Wha-at?*

EVE. He's been so patient—waiting all these years for people to learn how to live on the earth. So today—well, He just got tired and took everybody away!

MICHAEL (*aghast*). Eve!

EVE. Michael, don't look at me like that! Is what I said any more crazy than—than what's *happened?* Look—this street should be like daylight with electric signs! There should be so many people around us, and automobiles coming and going and street-cars and—and a whole city living! (*Wind sighs*) But there's nothing! Michael, who else but God could have taken them away? Why can't it be true? He got so tired of the horrible mess they were making of things that He—He took them away! Yes, that's it! He . . .

MICHAEL. No, stop it!

EVE. But, Michael . . .

MICHAEL. No, crazy talk . . . I won't listen!

EVE. Crazy because we don't understand!

MICHAEL. It's impossible, I tell you.

EVE. Why is it impossible? Michael, I don't know very much, but I know this: I've been thinking about it all the time we've been walking. Call the way people got here on earth any name you want, but, no matter how you say it, when you really think about it, it's all a miracle—things joining in the empty air and growing out of things that couldn't move, and the animals changing for millions of years until there were men. . . . I tell you, it's all crazy and impossible and yet someone made it happen, so why not *this?* Yes, if He made men, why couldn't He get tired of the way they were doing things and *destroy* them?

(*Wind sighs.*)

MICHAEL (*slowly*). I—I can't believe it's *you* talking.

EVE. Michael, I—I think I'm saying the truth! Someone made mankind—and that someone just destroyed them!

MICHAEL. Then what're *we* doing here! We're flesh and blood like the rest!

EVE. Maybe He just forgot us. (*Wind sighs*) Or maybe . . .

MICHAEL. What?

EVE. It doesn't matter!

MICHAEL. Tell me!

EVE. Maybe you and I . . .

MICHAEL. Well?

EVE. Maybe He wanted just a couple of people—to start over with.

(*Wind sighs.*)

MICHAEL (*slowly*). You say crazy things—and then you say crazier ones.

EVE. What if it's true, Michael? Think! What if it's true? The things you said up on the roof during the storm—the good things—maybe He heard them and liked them.

MICHAEL. Getting so dark.

EVE. Maybe He heard them and liked them.

MICHAEL. I'm awfully tired. . . . Let's find a place to sleep.

EVE. All right.

MICHAEL. Help you up . . . (*With effort*) Ah!

EVE. Where'll we go?

MICHAEL. Any place. We can go any place now.

EVE. Yes.

(*Sound of slow, echoing footsteps on sidewalk.*)

EVE. Let's hurry. . . . It'll be terrible on the streets when it's very dark.

(*Footsteps tempo increases.*)

MICHAEL. Yes!

EVE. No, wait, Michael!

(*Footsteps out with:*)

MICHAEL. Huh?

EVE. Why should we hurry and be afraid? Who can *harm* us *now?*

MICHAEL (*slowly*). You're right. All the—the harm is out of the city now.

EVE. Oh, Michael, you don't quite believe all the things I've said before, but tomorrow, when the sun's shining again and we really know that this happened and isn't a kind of a dream, you'll believe then, won't you, Michael?

MICHAEL. Maybe.

EVE. You're—you're thinking something—tell me what?

(*Music begins, continuing softly behind.*)

MICHAEL. If what you think *did* happen, maybe—maybe He left a few more people like us at different places on the earth—I mean plain ordinary people—to join together and make a new world. We'll have to help run things.

EVE. Michael, yes!

MICHAEL. But—but—we don't know anything about running a world, you and I! We're—we're just you and me! How can *we* do better than—than they did—the millions of them!

EVE (*slowly*). Maybe by—by remembering something they sort of forgot.

MICHAEL. What?

EVE. It's just to do unto others—as you would have them do unto you.

(*Musical curtain.*)

THE WOMEN STAYED AT HOME

And, after a while, you find yourself hating too much. The enemy has cloven feet and syphilitic breath. And then you remember the little people who, all through bloody history, have fought on the wrong side, and been told it was the right side. . . .

THE WOMEN STAYED AT HOME

ANNOUNCER. The scene: a wind-swept coast. It is night. For once the sea is calm. It waits ominously upon the edge of shore where sits a woman and an old man. For a long time they have sat quietly, but now the woman speaks to the old man, and her words lift out to the sea on the rush of the wind. . . .

(*Wind sighs.*)

(*Music: Opening of "Tristan and Isolde." Music continues behind.*)

CELIA. Lonely? (*Wind sighs*) Yes, I *was* lonely. And I did what I did because I was lonely. . . . I can tell you—this is a quiet place. My father built here because he and Mother had each other, and they wanted the lonesomeness. The village over there, and we away from all the rest—my father wanted it that way. . . . When I was very young, it was all right. I could run with the other children, and it was all right. But when I grew older it was lonely. The sea— the wind—the gulls flying—is that enough for a girl? Yes, I was very lonely. (*Church bells tolling far, far back*) Father died at sea. A storm—his boat . . . (*Church bells continue tolling*) Then Mother . . . For the first time I really *was* alone. . . . People who have nothing remember the little things they've had, don't they? I remember things so clearly. The way the clouds were one day when the sun went under. . . . A boat that stood out on the horizon and then in a second went under—the way so many of . . . No, why talk of that? Tell you of—John . . . He came to the village a month after Mother died. He had a pack on his back and a smile that lifted the heart. I met him right where we sit . . .

(*Music out.*)

(*Wind up slightly as transition, then fading out.*)

JOHN (*fade-in, cheerily*). Hello, girl!

CELIA (*startled*). Oh!

JOHN. Oh, I'm sorry if I startled you.

CELIA. I—I didn't know that. . . .

JOHN (*chuckling*). Yes, I know. My mother used to say it of me, too. I had a walk like a cat on tiptoe! Ah, it's a pleasant day!

CELIA. Yes, isn't it . . . ?

JOHN. Where are you from?

CELIA. That house. . . .

JOHN. Oh! It's a strange, lonely place to build a house, isn't it?

CELIA. Yes. . . .

JOHN. May I tell you my name? It's John Clark.

CELIA. How do you do?

JOHN. Would you tell me yours?

CELIA. Celia Harris.

JOHN. Celia! (*Excitedly*) There's a name! Yes, for my boat!

CELIA. W-what?

JOHN. Oh, oh—I beg your pardon! It's your name, isn't it? I've no right to use it!

CELIA. You said a boat!

JOHN. Yes—yes—*my* boat. I'm going to make a living at fishing; that's why I came here. And I've got a new boat. Well, not exactly new . . . And I've been beating out the inside of my head trying to think of a lucky name for it! Celia—it's a lovely name! (*Fade*) Do you mind if I tell you that? Do you mind?

(*Wind sighs down behind.*)

(*Music: "Tristan" behind.*)

CELIA. I didn't mind. . . . I didn't mind anything he told me. . . . (*Music out. Sound of happy laughter, etc., of villagers at wedding. Fiddler playing English folk dance all far, far back, continuing behind*) The village was so happy the day we married. It's good to remember. . . .

(*Laughter of villagers and fiddling up slowly continuing behind.*)

JOHN (*fade-in*). Cele.

CELIA. Yes, darling.

JOHN. Now's our chance!

CELIA. What . . . ?

JOHN. To get away from them!

CELIA. But, John!

JOHN. Shh! Quiet, now. Slip easy as a ghost around the corner—now, come on—run!

(*Fiddler down and fade out.*)

CELIA (*breathlessly, as she runs*). They'll never—forgive us!

JOHN. Go on! It's the dancin' and drinkin' that they're after! Come on—faster!

CELIA (*ad libs breathless remarks such as, "Oh, no!" "I can't!" etc., then, on cue*). Oh, no, John! No!

JOHN. Wha' . . . ?

(*Running out behind.*)

CELIA. I can't! Not another step! (*Breathing heavily*) It's beating so—my heart. . . .

JOHN (*as he takes her close in his arms*). *My* heart!

CELIA (*in close*). John. . . .

JOHN. I want you. . . .

CELIA. I'm yours. . . .

JOHN. Always mine. (*Fade fast*) Always mine. . . .

(*Wind as transition, down and intermittently behind.*)

(*Music: "Tristan" behind.*)

CELIA. Always mine—he said that—always mine. (*Building*) Tell me, how long is always? I want to know. I wanted to know then. I want to know now! Is always the moment he held me and his lips were tight on mine and his arms held me and he . . . (*Music out. Breaks off, recovers self, down, slowly*) No. Why should I ask? I really know. Always, with him, was that night. Because the next night . . .

(*Fade-in sound of surf, boat sound continuing behind.*)

JOHN (*off slightly, calling*). Cast off!

VOICE No. 1 (*back*). Cast off!

VOICE No. 2 (*further back*). Aye, aye!

VOICE No. 1 (*back*). Good-bye!

God go with you!

Good luck! (*Etc., ad lib.*)

JOHN. Celia! Good-bye, darlin'! I'll be thinking about you! And I'll bring a good catch home for you! I'll see you in a fortnight, darlin'! (*Fade*) Just in a fortnight! Fortnight!

(*Music: "Tristan" behind.*)

(*Wind sighing behind.*)

CELIA (*flat, dull voice*). He said that to me; but in a fortnight he was . . .

VOICE (*whispering*). Dead . . .

CELIA. I think it. I can't say it. It's been so long, and yet I can only think it. . . .

VOICE (*fade whispering*). Dead . . .

CELIA. Do you know what that meant?

(*Music out.*)

(*Fade-in the slow, doleful chiming of church bells together with:*)

MINISTER. We have come here to say the last words for the

soul of the one whom the sea has taken to the Lord. Good-bye, John Clark. The Lord in His wisdom has buried you in the boundless grave of the ocean. We bow our heads and we weep our tears. (*Fade*) We have the memory of you, the sea has your body, and the Lord your soul. . . . Blessed are they that mourn you, for they shall be comforted. . . .

(*Wind softly behind.*)

(*Music: "Tristan" behind.*)

CELIA. Do you know what that meant? I was alone again! Yes, alone again!

VOICES (*back, fading fast*). The Widow Clark—the Widow Clark—(*Fade*) the Widow Clark—the Widow Clark. . . .

CELIA. I ran from the village—away—away from them—back up the long path to my house. And all the way it was tearing in me—I was alone again! Alone again! But a new loneliness—a horrible loneliness. When you've had nothing, all right, you *know* nothing! But I'd known *something* now: his look—his laugh—his lips—his arms—the crush of his arms . . . (*Breaks down and cries. Cries herself out then, simply*) I was alone again. . . . (*Music, slow, dead, foreboding, behind*) A day—and a night—a day—and a night—one after the other. An empty day—after an empty night . . . That's what was ahead of me. And that's what I had. An empty day—and an empty night—an empty day —and an empty night—over and over and over . . . And there was no end—there could be no end to it—until there was an end of me! (*Slowly, softly*) No end to it until there was an end of me! And then . . .

(*Music out.*)

(*Rumble of drum behind.*)

VOICE (*far back, shouting*). War!

(*Drum fade-out.*)

CELIA. I heard it from far down the village. I couldn't quite understand. One of the men waving his arms at me and shouting . . .

(*Drum behind.*)

VOICE (*in a little closer*). War! We're at war!

(*Drum fade-out.*)

CELIA. War? War? But everyone has said—but, wait! If war had come there would be something for me to do! Yes! Fill the emptiness in me with something to do! Yes!

VILLAGER (*back—the pompousness of the small-time official*). I'm sorry, Widow Clark, but there's nothing for you to do! Everything's being taken care of in the proper manner. (*Fade*) Sorry, Widow Clark, there's nothing for you to do. . . .

(*Wind sighs.*)

CELIA. Nothing for me to do . . . Nothing—for me . . .

(*Drum.*)

VOICES (*far back*). War! War! War! War! (*Fading*) War! War!

(*Drum fade.*)

CELIA. Nothing . . .

(*Marching feet fading quickly.*)

CELIA. For me . . .

(*Murmur of voices back and continuing behind.*)

VOICES. Navy'll blockade 'em!
  Do our duty!
  Naval battles!
  Submarines!
  Army!
  Navy!

CELIA (*on cue through above*). But nothing for me . . . War means something to those that have something to live for, to fight for. . . . But when you have nothing . . . (*Music: Same monotonous, slow, "Tristan" measures behind*) Empty days after empty nights—over again—over again . . . And again I began to think . . .

VOICE (*whispering*). No end to it, until there is an end to me. . . .

CELIA. Why not? Walk into the sea . . . Let the sea fill my emptiness, cover my loneliness, why not? *Why not?* I left the house and walked toward the sea. (*Sound: Walking in sand far back behind*) The sand crushed beneath my feet the way it did that night—*he* ran with me. . . . (*Sound: Of surf faintly behind*) The water was dark. . . . (*Actual sound of water behind*) I was at the edge, and, into it, (*Splashing down behind*) deeper and deeper into it. . . . Cold against me—cold, as the days and the nights. . . . But this coldness would end, and with that ending put a finish to the ache in me. And then something touched me! I looked down. White in the water—a hand!

(*Music out cold.*)

VOICE (*back—echo*). John!

CELIA (*quickly*). The thought echoing in my head, and then . . . No, no, a stranger—someone . . . I dragged him out of the water to the beach. (*Splashing sounds out behind the above*) A stranger, drowned in the sea—dead—yes . . . (*Begin to fade-in sound of heartbeat*) But no—my ear against the wet of him—his heart—yes, the beat of it—faint, but the beat of it . . . (*Heartbeat grows stronger slowly behind*) Dragged him, carried him to the house . . . Warmed him—hour after hour—and slowly the beat lifted with the blood in him, stronger and stronger. . . . (*Fade heartbeat—cross-fade sound of birds, hold for a few seconds, then fade behind*) Morning. He opened his eyes. In the first light of

the sun I saw they were blue—as blue as John's had
been. . . .

(*Fade-in heavy breathing of the man.*)

(CARL *moans unintelligibly.*)

(*Rumble of kettledrum back and growing behind.*)

CELIA. His first words! What . . . ?

(CARL *moans again.*)

CELIA. Who . . . I ran to where I had thrown the clothes. The
buttons—words on them . . . He was—he was—(*Drum
out cold*) the *enemy!* (*Down tensely*) Enemy! I knew
what I had to do. Go down to the village, say . . . (*Up*)
Listen, everybody! A man from an enemy boat! I've got
him—caught him! Come and get him! (*Down*) An enemy!
Come and get him! I went back to where he lay. He was
sleeping now. Sleeping. I looked at him . . . Something
twisted in my heart. He slept the way John had slept that
night—head in the crook of his arm, sandy hair curling
down on a forehead smooth and brown. He slept that
night . . .

VOICE (*far back, echo*). Listen, everybody! An enemy!

CELIA. Yes. I must tell *them*. I must. . . . (*Wind sighs softly*)
He slept. Woke for a few hours—then slept again . . . Let
him sleep, I told myself. There would be time to tell *them*
—tomorrow. (*Wind sighs*) But I didn't tell them—tomorrow. He was sick. I had to make him well. *Then* I would
tell them. How many days went? I don't remember. All I
remember is moments . . .

(*Fade-in sound of bird singing, continuing behind.*)

(CARL *tries to say "bird."*)

CELIA (*fade-in*). What did you say?

(CARL *tries to say word.*)

CELIA. No, no! That's a bird. Bird . . .

CARL (*tries the word*). Bird . . .

CELIA. That's very good! Pretty bird!

CARL (*imitates her*). Pretty bird! (*Fade*) Pretty bird . . .
(*Sound of singing bird fades with above fade; wind sighs.*)

CELIA. So I began to teach him how to speak my language.

CARL (*back*). I . . . You . . . Me . . . Water . . . Sea . . .

CELIA (*on cue through above*). Why not? I wanted him to
speak the way I do.

CARL (*back*). Day . . . Night . . . I am hungry. I want to
sleep.

CELIA (*on cue through above*). In the prison camp it would
help him to know our language. So I taught him . . .

CARL (*fade-in on cue*). I am Carl. I am Carl. I am Carl.

CELIA. Good! Good! Now try something else!

CARL. I am Carl. You are—you are . . .

CELIA. Celia. Say, "How do you do, Celia?"

CARL. How are you do, Celia . . . ?

CELIA. No! No! How *do* you do?

CARL. How *do* you do, Celia? I am Carl. (*Fade*) I am Carl.
(*Wind sighs.*)

CELIA. Soon he was well enough to be up and about. I gave
him a suit of John's to wear. He would sit in the window,
looking out at the sea, and I would work. . . .

(CARL *fade-in whistling old folk song, hold back behind.*)

CELIA. And listen to him. . . .

(CARL *continues to whistle folk song back behind.*)

CELIA. It was good to—know that someone was there. . . .

(*Fade* CARL'S *whistling slowly.*)

(*Music behind.*)

CELIA. Suddenly I realized something! *I wasn't lonely any
more!* Not lonely! Can you understand what that means?
To have had nothing, and then—to have something! Some-

one to talk to, to listen to, to laugh with . . . (*Music cuts cold*) To . . . (*Stops suddenly.*)

(*Murmur of voices back behind.*)

VOICES (*back*). Naval battles!

> Submarines!
>
> Army!
>
> Navy!
>
> War!
>
> Army!
>
> Navy!

CELIA. But I had to tell *them!* I *had* to! Had to? And then I began to ask myself, "Why?" What had I to do with war? What had I to do with enemies?

OFFICIAL'S VOICE (*back—fade slowly*). Sorry, Widow Clark, there's nothing for you to do! Everything's being taken care of in the proper manner! (*Fade out*) Sorry, Widow Clark, there's nothing for you to do!

CARL (*back*). Celia, you are very good to me. . . .

CELIA. He was no enemy to me—just—Carl. And his eyes were blue. . . . And his face was gentle. . . . And when he smiled his lips . . . No, how could I tell them? And then . . . (*Vigorous knocking on door, back*) It happened!

(*Fade-in knocking on door.*)

CARL (*whispering*). Celia, who—who is . . .

CELIA (*whispering*). I don't know! No one ever comes up here!

(*Knocking again.*)

CARL. You must answer . . .

CELIA. Hide!

CARL. No—trouble—the police—they will . . .

CELIA. Hide, I tell you! Quickly!

(*Fade-in knocking on door fuller—out with opening door.*)

VILLAGER (*pompous official, off slightly*). Well—well—well! I'd begun to wonder if you were home!

CELIA. Oh, Mr. Stanford! What—do you want?

VILLAGER. Want? Want? Now, there's a question! Climb all the way up that infernal path, and you look at me as if I brought you bad news! Well, I don't, and that's a fact!

CELIA. Well . . .

VILLAGER. I'll tell you plain enough! A chance to do your duty . . . Yes—and I'm the one who's fixed it for you!

CELIA. What . . . ?

VILLAGER. What—what—have you no other word but what? Your duty in this war, of course! The district teacher's off to join his regiment! Come down to the district schoolhouse three times a week and teach the children! (*Fading*) A chance to do your duty, Widow Clark, for God and country!

(*Wind sighs.*)

CELIA. For God and country . . . Teach the children . . . Come down to the schoolhouse . . . Leave *him*!

CARL (*fade-in*). I will be all right, Celia—go. . . . (*Fade*) I will be all right.

CELIA. So I went down to the village again. (*Fade-in murmur of voices behind*) And heard of many things down there in the village . . .

(*Up with murmur.*)

VOICES. They're drowning our men!
They're swamping the lifeboats!
They're killing our men!
They're killing our sons!
They're killing our lovers!
They're killing our husbands!

CELIA (*through above cries*). *They—they—they . . . Who?*

Yes, the enemy! Drowning and bombing and killing—*they* —*they*—*they*! (*Down tensely*) The enemy! All day long— all I heard—the enemy! (*The cries of the villagers fade out*) I climbed the path back to the house at sundown. . . . He was waiting. . . .

CARL (*fade-in*). Celia, I am very—happy—to—see you. . . .

CELIA. I said nothing. What could I say? We ate. It grew dark. He didn't speak again—just looked at me. . . . (*Music slow, foreboding, begins*) And then, suddenly, it was as if he were gone—as if I had told them and he had been taken away! I was alone again—alone again and— lonely. No one near me—no one to talk to—the emptiness of the days again. . . . (*Music out. Weeps*) No, no, I couldn't go back to that, I couldn't! (*Wind sighs*) The next day, down to the village again. I wouldn't listen this time, I told myself. . . . (*Fade-in small boy crying, hold back behind*) But in the schoolhouse . . .

(*Small boy in a little closer, weeping.*)

SMALL GIRL (*fade-in*). It's his brother, ma'am. On the boat *they* torpedoed yesterday. (*Fade*) It's his only brother, ma'am.

(*Small boy in close, weeping, fade.*)

CELIA. *They* again . . . (*Building*) *They* again! *They again!*

(*Murmur of* VILLAGERS.)

VOICES (*off*). They're drowning our men!
       They're killing our sons!
       They're killing our fathers!
       They're killing our sons!
       They!
       They! They! They! (*Fade*) They! They! They!

CELIA (*on cue through preceding speech*). No! No! I turned, I ran! Away from them! *They! They!* No more *they's!* He was only one! Only one! And he was in my house! And he was in my heart! All right, I said it! (*Tears in voice*) In my heart! (*Wind sighs. Quiet love music of "Tristan" begins behind*) He spoke to me that night. . . .

CARL (*fade-in*). Celia—Celia—I want to say something to you, *bitte.* . . .

CELIA. Yes, Carl.

CARL. You are not—happy.

CELIA. No. . . .

CARL. It is—me . . . I know. I am . . .

CELIA. Carl—please.

CARL. If I—could speak well—enough—to tell you . . .

CELIA. What . . . ?

CARL. That all these days I have been with you I have been thinking—and I have been learning—that what you and your people think is right. And, because it is right—it will live. I know that now. And so the hate is not ours—not yours—not mine.

CELIA (*weeping softly*). Oh, Carl . . .

CARL. Oh, Celia! Not yours—not mine!

CELIA. I love you, Carl. (*In close*) I love you, Carl! (*Music out. Wind sighs*) So I said it. And his arms came close around me . . . And there was no earth or sky or death. . . . (*"Tristan" music begins, sensuously beautiful, continuing behind. Slowly, in memory of love*) The days after that? Days that stood still in wonder—and then in rush were gone. Warm days—lazy days—wonderful days—days when the sky reached down and lifted us to the clouds, and we . . . Oh, Carl . . . Carl . . . (*Wind sighs*) And then a new day—a morning—sun awakened me—stretched out my hand . . . (*Off mike, sharply*) Carl! No! Carl! Carl, where are you? (*Building*) Carl, where are you? (*Up, crying out*

137

—echo chamber. Music out) Carl! (*Down*) Gone—gone—
I cried . . . Not very long . . . You see, I understood. Always, in our days together, there'd been a cloud, and with
each passing day that cloud would have grown larger and
larger until there was no warmth of sun for us. The cloud
of fear—that someone of the village would see us—see him
—and seeing him—end my world for me. And he knew
that . . . And so he went away. . . . (*Music: "Tristan"
behind*) Where? I don't know. I like to think he took a
boat during the night and sailed out to sea in it back to
where he came from . . . Back to *his* small village by the
cliffs . . . I like to think that . . . I know some day the
fighting will be over. It must end. He said it . . .

CARL (*in close, whispering*). And so the hate is not ours—
not yours—not mine . . .

CELIA. It will end. He'll come back to me. I'll never be lonely
any more. . . .

(*Musical curtain.*)

AN AMERICAN IS BORN

I had always felt that a playwright who adapts published stories or novels to the radio medium was either sterile or lazy and was trying to get a corner of his bread into someone else's gravy bowl.

I got off my fine horse when I read Dalton Trumbo's amazing Johnny Got His Gun. *The story of a blind, deaf, dumb, armless, legless, living relic of World War No. 1 was made for the radio medium. Although the average dramatization of a novel loses some of its meaning when compressed to capsule radio size,* Johnny Got His Gun *had even greater emotional impact on the air because the thoughts transformed into living speech became almost unendurable reality.*

When it came to picking a radio "Johnny," the logical choice was the red-haired cinema portrayer of the average "who-ya-shovin'" Americano, James Cagney.

For the munificent sum of $21 (the union minimum), Jimmy proceeded to put in a week of rehearsals intensive enough to make us both wish that Mrs. Trumbo had never had a son.

Before rehearsals, of course, there was the little matter of writing the radio play. As usual, I procrastinated writing until the day before the rehearsal, and then worked straight through until dawn finishing it.

The network time given us amounted to twenty-nine minutes, thirty seconds. In the first rehearsal I found that I had written a play that ran exactly one hour and ten minutes. I think that long version was a good play, but, in order to

140

broadcast it, it would have meant the cancellation of two or three crunchy-munchy and boasty-toasty epics, so another all-through-the-night session took place while the dialogue was whittled down to half-hour size.

There is a great illusion that when a writer cuts his own work, each lopped-off adjective drips with the gore of his anguish. I believe that's nonsense. A professional writer quickly discovers that the most effective things he has to say are those which are left unsaid. The magic of good writing, and particularly good writing for the radio, comes about through the contribution of the listener's imagination.

So I did little weeping over the hour version of Johnny as I hacked away with blue pencil and stop-watch.

Practically everyone who has ever damned Hollywood has in the second breath applauded the creative ingenuity of the technical motion-picture crafts—cameras, sound, properties and special effects.

That same technical creativeness holds true in radio, and was brought home to me during the Johnny broadcast; one of the potent parts of the book is when the blind, deaf and dumb soldier learns to recognize the approach of the nurse by the vibrations of her footsteps coming up through the bedsprings and reacting against his skin. It's not so difficult to say in words "he could feel the vibrations," but to put across the same idea in one-dimensional radio, without the use of narrators, is another matter.

I gave the tall order to NBC's sound-effects department. On the first try, they (Saz and Padgett) came up with perfection. If you heard the broadcast, you remember that eerie vibratory something which happened every time we heard Johnny thinking about the approach of the nurse. The effect that twisted your insides was accomplished by touching a metal rod, at one end of which a crystal microphone was attached, against a vibrating door-spring.

But to come back to adaptations: through Johnny, and subsequent adaptations of Somerset Maugham's Of Human Bondage, Eric Knight's The Flying Yorkshireman, as well as the play which follows, I changed my mind, first, as to whether adapting another man's material was the lazy road and, second, as to the effectiveness of translating a story from one medium to another. Making over another man's story into a radio play is a typewriter full of work—if one is actually concerned about writing a radio play. Approaches must be found that will get the listener into the story quickly and sustain his interest; these technics and devices must be devised to substitute for the slower, lengthier approach of the novel or stage play. That means work. That means as much mental and physical trial and error as the creation of an original play from an original idea. More, perhaps, because with one's own pattern one can cut and trim; such freedom with an established work would result in mayhem by the original author or author's agent.

And yet, one must not hew too closely to the creator's line in adaptation; there must be sufficient daring to redirect not basic plot lines, but settings and approaches. Any dramatic work used on the radio should be rewritten for radio.

In adapting the classic, Of Human Bondage, to the air, I spent a month trying to write a play following the exact line of the novel. After exhausting two quires of paper and three typewriters, I was a fit candidate for a producer's padded cell. It's a skyscraper order to try to tell the story of Philip's childhood, his youth, all his relationships, the Mildred story, and the rest of it within a 29.45 minute time schedule. The fact that Bette Davis was the star of my broadcast, of course, *suggested the idea of telling the story from Mildred's stand-point. That solved the problem of approach, but it didn't take care of giving the story unity and direction and meaning since, if only the Mildred story were told, but a single facet of Maugham's novel would be given the audience.*

The solution was a simple one—after a month's work: to tell the story through Mildred's eyes, but tell it in such a manner that one saw the lie behind her story. The plan, then, was this: Mildred, at the end of her life, is pleading her case to a priest at her bedside, and, after each of her self-righteous statements, we show what really *happened between Philip and herself, climaxed by her final confession; the result was movement and unification, the twin necessities of good radio story-telling.*

I stay with the business of adaptations this long because my inner ears are tired of being abused by half-hearted on-the-line adaptations of classics which are actually not radio adaptations at all, but novels or stage plays with narrators stuck on fore and aft to let the audience know the parts that the adapter was too lazy or too inept to reform into the radio medium.

An American Is Born *which follows is an adaptation of a novella by Peter Jefferson Packer and Fanya Foss. Elisabeth Bergner played the lead—her first radio broadcast. Miss Bergner is another lady who has a reputation for eating directors' hearts without salt. Other than the fact that she asked to be permitted to broadcast while sitting down—for fear that her trembling legs would collapse under her—the rehearsals and broadcast went on quite uneventfully, except for a heightened first-night tension.*

Sitting in the control-room I could feel the contagious nervousness of the atmosphere and so, as a safety valve, I spoke through the microphone which is the director's com-munication between the sound-proof control-room into the studio.

I told a very lengthy and very bad joke badly. I came to the very dull conclusion and waited. There was an embarrassed silence on the other side of the plate-glass.

And then Miss Bergner, looking around at the silent actors and sound men and musicians, said very softly, "Please, will someone laugh so we can go on with the rehearsal?"

Anyway, it was a good broadcast.

AN AMERICAN IS BORN

(*Music: Behind.*)

ANNOUNCER. The place: the border between United States and Mexico. An archway across the street—the words on it glint sharply in the sunshine—"Entering Mexico." A man and a woman stand there, backs to the American side, eyes on the sun-baked road into Mexico. They are Karl and Marta Kroft: young, eager and impatient.

(*Music: Up and fade-out.*)

MARTA. Karl.

KARL. Yes?

MARTA. With the left foot first, please. That means we'll be back soon.

KARL. All right.

MARTA. One, two, three—go!

(*We hear the sound in the roadway as they jump across the line.*)

MARTA (*laughter in voice*). There! Now we are in Mexico!

KARL. Not for long, I hope.

MARTA. It looks romantic.

KARL. Not to me. Anyway, Mexicali is only a border town— a—a hybrid.

MARTA. Whatever it is, it is only for a few days, so don't look so unhappy, my darling.

VOICE (*Mexican, back*). *Amigos!* You register in here! This way!

KARL. Oh! Oh, yes, of course! (*Sotto, to* MARTA) Some more infernal questions and signatures and explanations!

(*Door off slightly.*)

Voice (*back*). In here.

Karl. Careful—the step.

Marta. I'm all right.

Voice No. 2 (*back slightly*). Names, please.

Karl. Karl Kroft. This is my wife, Marta.

Voice No. 2 (*flatly, declaratively*). Not Americans.

Karl. No. Czecho-Slovakian.

Voice No. 2. Your passports, please.

Karl. Yes, of course. I had them. Yes, there you are.

Marta (*sotto, quickly*). Trouble, Karli?

Karl. No, no, just formalities.

Marta. Oh. . . .

Voice No. 2. And what is your reason for coming to Mexico, Señor Kroft?

Karl (*hesitantly*). Well, well, you see—uh—we . . .

Voice No. 2. Speak up, señor.

Marta. No, *I* will tell you.

Karl. Marta . . .

Marta. No! Why shouldn't I tell him the truth? You see, sir, the reason we have come to Mexico is because I am going to . . . Well—(*In a rush*) you see, I want my son to be born an American!

Voice No. 2 (*slowly*). So you come to *Mexico?*

Marta. Karli—*you* tell him.

Karl. We are here because they told us it is the fastest way to get back into America officially. I am an engineer, and my wife and I came here from Prague because I had to do work on my country's exhibit at the New York World's Fair.

Marta. But we could not go back to Prague. We do not *want* to go back *now,* and the American officials told us that if we want to stay in America and become citizens, first we must leave the country and come back in again under the quota law.

KARL. They told us that Mexico was the nearest foreign country which was willing to grant temporary residence to aliens while they waited for their immigration papers to be arranged. That is why we are here.

MARTA. Yes.

VOICE No. 2. So . . . I will stamp your passports. (*Sound of stamping twice*) Karl and Marta Kroft, may you enjoy your stay in Mexico.

KARL. Thank you.

MARTA. Thank you very much. You are very kind, but you understand we can only stay here a few days. (*In quietly, intensely*) We *must* get back to America.

(*Musical transition. Board fade-in.* MARTA *and* KARL *laughing.*)

KARL (*laughing, imitating Mexican hotel-keeper*). Ze best room in ze house!

(*Goes off into gales of laughter.*)

MARTA (*still laughing*). Hot and cold running water, if you run for it!

KARL. A bath in every room—if you climb in the washbowl! (*They laugh, then:*) It's pretty terrible, isn't it?

MARTA. Oh, Karl, what's the difference? Today is Wednesday. I'm sure we'll be back in Los Angeles on Saturday.

KARL. You're very wonderful!

MARTA. No. . . .

KARL. Your skin is so cool and sweet. . . .

MARTA. Karli, I was just wondering what part of America we ought to live in when we get back.

KARL. Any place that has a garden and trees and a river close by where he can learn to swim.

MARTA. Who?

KARL. You know. . . .

MARTA (*chuckles softly*). And if he turns out to be a young lady?

KARL. Then she'll be a lovely little mermaid, like her mother. Oh, my little Marta. . . .

MARTA (*in close, in his arms*). Karl. . . . (*Piano starts playing Strauss waltz far, far back*) Karl, listen!

KARL. Eh?

MARTA. A Strauss waltz! Listen!

KARL (*listening*). But there should be mandolins here, not Strauss waltzes!

MARTA. I thought I never wanted to hear . . . Let's go see who it is!

KARL (*fade*). All right.

(*Sound of opening door. Music builds behind above sound effects.*)

MARTA. Look at the people listening! Karl, let's go back.

KARL. No! No—we will meet them.

(*Music up to end of piece. Sprinkling of applause by three people.*)

DR. CASPAR. Bravo, Franz! You play beautifully!

FRANZ. Thank you, Doctor, but I see we have visitors. How do you do? My name is Franz Bruckner.

KARL (*fade-in*). How do you do? Forgive us for intruding. My name is Kroft—Karl Kroft. This is my wife.

FRANZ. How do you do, Mrs. Kroft?

MARTA. You play beautifully.

FRANZ. Thank you. May I present Dr. and Mrs. Caspar?

(*There is a murmur of "How-do-you-do's."*)

MARTA. It's moving to hear that music again, don't you think so, Mrs.—uh—Caspar?

MRS. CASPAR. It is lovely until he stops, then it is a bitter echo in the ears.

FRANZ (*flatly, after tense silence*). I—I am very tired. I will go to bed. Good night, Mr. and Mrs. Kroft. (*Fade*) Good night, Doctor—Mrs. Caspar.

(*There is a murmur of "good nights." We hear sound of* FRANZ *going upstairs far in background, his footsteps fading out.*)

DOCTOR. Please, Mr. and Mrs. Kroft, won't you sit down?

KARL. Thank you.

MARTA. Thank you very much.

DOCTOR. This chair—Mrs. Kroft, it is the most comfortable.

MARTA. But you were sitting there.

DOCTOR. No, I think *you* had better sit in it. (*Chuckles*) Don't blush! After all, I *am* a doctor.

MARTA. Yes.

DOCTOR. So! Now we are all comfortable—as comfortable as we can be here.

MRS. CASPAR. This is a poor excuse for a hotel, isn't it, Mrs. Kroft?

MARTA. Thank goodness we'll be out by the end of the week.

DOCTOR. Out?

KARL. She means back in America.

DOCTOR. What makes you so sure? You are here to get your quota number, aren't you?

MARTA. Yes, we are, but it will not take us more than a day or two, and then we are in America for good. May I ask where you and Mrs. Caspar are from?

MRS. CASPAR. We are from Vienna.

MARTA. Oh! So you, too, are waiting for your quota number.

DOCTOR. We are.

MARTA. And how long have you been here?

DOCTOR (*slowly*). How long have we been here, *liebchen?*

MRS. CASPAR. We have been here fourteen months.

MARTA (*unbelievingly*). Fourteen months! But—but why?

KARL. Yes! Why so long, Doctor?

DOCTOR. Quota numbers, my dear Mr. and Mrs. Kroft. Somewhere down the long list of immigrants who look to America for salvation you will find our names. Some day the magic finger will point to us. Meanwhile we wait.

KARL. We—we had no idea, Doctor. I mean . . .

DOCTOR. No, no, do not apologize. It is very hot here—very uncomfortable—but we wait.

MRS. CASPAR. We wait—as all must wait.

MARTA. No—no, it can't be true! We won't have to wait so long! We *can't* wait so long! We can't . . .

KARL (*through above*). Marta, please, you mustn't excite yourself.

MARTA (*recovering self*). I—I'm sorry.

DOCTOR. No, we are the ones who are sorry. We had no right to alarm you so needlessly. We hope sincerely that neither one of you will have any difficulty returning to the United States, eh, *liebchen?*

MRS. CASPAR (*flatly*). We hope sincerely.

(*Musical transition.*)

CONSUL (*fade-in*). Yes, indeed, as the American Consul, I can say without contradiction that we have some very nice people waiting for their quota numbers. Dr. Caspar and his wife . . . Franz Bruckner—poor Franz—unfortunately, his wife and his children are still in Europe. By the way, if you're staying at the Border Hotel, I'd advise you to take a room on the north side. The ventilation in that place is not all it should be.

MARTA (*through dry lips*). Mr. Consul, the one thing we want to know you have not told us. We have been here a week—how much longer must we stay?

CONSUL. It is really difficult to say. I must ask you to have patience.

MARTA. Patience?

KARL. Can't you tell us something definite, Mr. Consul? There is a particular reason why we should get back to the States as soon as possible.

CONSUL. Mr. Kroft—Mrs. Kroft—America is doing what it can. Our quota laws were designed to take care of as many people as America could absorb without jeopardizing the economic life of the country. We have given refuge to many who might be excluded, were it not for a liberal interpretation of the law. Though our sympathy for the unfortunate in other countries is profound, all must take their turn. I can say nothing more definite than that. I'm sorry. May I advise you to have patience and keep out of the sun as much as possible? The next month, and the month after that, August, are the worst we have down here.

MARTA (*softly*). August—my baby.

CONSUL. Did you say something, Mrs. Kroft?

MARTA. No, nothing. . . .

(*Musical transition.*)

MARTA (*strongly, firmly*). Patience.

(*Single harp string plucked, vibrates, then cuts sharply with:*)

KARL (*fade-in fast*). We can't get any of our money out of Prague—not a cent! (*Fade*) Our money, and they won't let us take a penny of it!

MARTA (*a little less certainly*). Patience.

(*Single harp string plucked, vibrates, then cuts sharply with:*)

KARL (*fade-in*). It's been three weeks, Marta—three weeks! The consul says that he doesn't know. (*Fade*) He doesn't know.

MARTA (*flatly*). Patience.

(*Single harp string plucked, vibrates, then cuts sharply with:*)

KARL (*fade-in*). I've tried, believe me, Marta, I've tried. But there's no work here—nothing! (*Fade*) Five weeks and I can't do anything for you.

(*Single harp string plucked, vibrates, then cuts sharply with:*)

MARTA (*starts the word slowly and then repeats it more rapidly, intensely*). Patience! Patience! Patience! Patience! Patience! (*Gets control of herself*) No, no, wait . . . I must wait . . . I must . . . I must—always wait. . . .

HOLST (*fade-in*). Come now, Mrs. Kroft—you sit in the corner of the veranda and talk to yourself.

MARTA (*looks up, tries to recover self*). I—I don't know you.

HOLST. My name is Holst. I am a resident of Mexicali for many years. Importer—exporter. Can I be of help to you?

MARTA. No, no, thank you.

HOLST. No, no, please do not go. You see, I, too, lived for many years in Prague.

MARTA. Oh, did you?

HOLST. Yes. As you see, I am not a Czecho-Slovakian, but Prague is very dear to me. Beautiful city, Prague.

MARTA. Yes—beautiful.

HOLST. How bitter it must be for you—this endless waiting! Tell me—perhaps I knew your family—what was your name before you were married?

MARTA. My name was Cernak.

HOLST. So? Was there not a Cernak in the Masaryk administration?

MARTA. My father.

HOLST. Indeed! Your father was a great democrat, Mrs. Kroft.

MARTA. Yes. He still is.

HOLST. Oh, he is still in Prague?

MARTA. Yes.

HOLST. Did he want you to come here? Please tell me!

MARTA. Well, my father always told me that the constitution of our little country was patterned on the American democracy. He told me that to visit America was to visit the fountainhead of democracy.

HOLST. Ah! How sad he is still in Europe, and now *you* wait to enter America to become a citizen. . . . You do not answer. Yes, I know—the waiting is endless. (*In close*) If you will listen to me, Mrs. Kroft, perhaps I can help.

MARTA. Help? But—but how? How is that possible?

HOLST. With money it is possible. Two hundred and fifty dollars.

MARTA. Our chance would come—sooner?

HOLST. *If* you trust me. . . . Well, why do you hesitate? Do you want to sit here and wait?

MARTA. It's just that—that I can't believe—such good luck. . . .

HOLST. I am always glad to do what I can. You will bring me the money?

MARTA. Yes! Oh, yes!

(*Musical transition.*)

MARTA (*she is singing or humming a Czecho-Slovakian folk-song as she sews. She cuts off as door opens back*). Karl!

KARL (*in fast*). What's this? The little *haus-frau* sewing again?

MARTA. Awful, isn't it?

KARL. Your hemstitching will be shown in museums for centuries.

(MARTA laughs.)

KARL. So good to hear you laugh.

MARTA. Oh, darling, I'm so happy. Did you see Mr. Holst?

KARL. He wasn't in his office.

MARTA. Oh, well, it's only been a week. I am sure we will hear from him any moment.

KARL (*uncertainly*). Yes—yes, of course we will.

MARTA (*quietly*). Karl, before we gave him all that money, we *did* investigate. Franz and Dr. Caspar—both of them said the man had influence—importance . . . (*Sudden knocking on door, back*) Karl! Our quota numbers . . .

KARL (*fade*). I'll go!

(*Door opening, back.*)

VOICE (*back*). *Por* Señorita.

KARL (*back*). Thank you. Here.

VOICE (*back*). *Gracias.*

(*Door closing, back.*)

MARTA. Karl! What is it?

KARL (*fade-in, puzzled*). Cablegram—for you.

MARTA. Cablegram? Give it to me!

KARL (*doubtfully*). Yes. . . .

(*Sound of tearing, crinkle of paper.*)

MARTA. Oh! It's from Anita! It says: (*Reads flatly, quickly*) "Your father very ill. (*She stops, then slowly*) In concentration camp."

KARL. Marta!

MARTA. I—am all right.

KARL. We'll—we'll do something.

MARTA. Mr. Holst!

KARL. Eh?

MARTA. Take me to Mr. Holst, Karl!

(*Musical transition.*)

HOLST. It is an unfortunate business.

MARTA. Mr. Holst, my father—he is an old man! Getting to America, my child—nothing means anything to me if I cannot help my father!

HOLST. Mr. Kroft, you have money?

KARL. All we have left in the world is two hundred dollars.

HOLST. What I must do will cost five hundred dollars.

MARTA. But, please . . .

KARL. But all we have is . . .

HOLST. Yes, I heard! It does not matter. I will advance you the money out of my personal funds. You can go home now. Your father will be all right.

MARTA. Oh, Karl, you hear! All right—everything is going to be all right! He will help my father and in a few days we will be in America. Oh, Karl, Karl!

KARL (*gently*). I know, little one . . .

HOLST. Good-bye. You will hear from me soon.

KARL (*fade*). Do not cry any more, Marta. Everything is all right now.

(*Door back.*)

HOLST (*up, curtly*). Heinrich!

VOICE (*back*). Yes, sir.

HOLST. Come here! Quickly!

VOICE (*in close*). Yes, Mr. Holst.

HOLST. A cablegram to the Secret Police in Prague—the usual code. "Dispose of Clemente Cernak case as is best for interest of the State. Relatives here are without influence or funds." Sign my name. That is all.

(*Musical transition.*)

(*Wind sighs gently, continuing intermittently behind.*)

KARL. We should go back to the hotel.

MARTA. No—let me sit here a little longer.

KARL. Still dizzy?

MARTA. I think that our son is getting impatient.

KARL. Should I call Dr. Caspar?

MARTA (*laughs softly*). No. Believe me, it's not going to happen here. It will be happen in America. Tell me, Karl, they say people born west of the Rockies are still pioneers. Does that mean he, too, will be a pioneer?

KARL. Your face grows lovelier every day.

MARTA (*chuckles softly*). I am lucky. . . .

FRANZ (*calling*). Hallo!

KARL. Who in the . . . ?

MARTA. Why, it's Franz.

KARL (*calls*). Here we are, Franz Bruckner.

FRANZ (*fading-in breathlessly*). Karl! Marta! Such news! Such news!

KARL. What?

MARTA. What is it, Franz?

FRANZ. My quota number! Tomorrow I can go into America!

KARL (*happily*). Franz!

MARTA (*joyously*). Franz, how wonderful!

FRANZ (*beside himself with joy*). I'll be able to bring over my wife and my children. We'll be together! Oh, God, how I've waited!

MARTA. Franz, we're so happy for you!

FRANZ. And you've got to be happy *with* me! Come—to the café!

KARL. What?

MARTA. Why?

FRANZ. We'll celebrate! It's a wonderful day, and it'll be a wonderful night!

MARTA. Yes, wonderful!

(*Musical transition.*)

156

AN AMERICAN IS BORN

(*Board fade-in sound of crowd at Aztec Inn. Music: a four-piece band is playing an old swing number. All down and continuing far back behind.*)

KARL. Enjoying yourself, darling?

MARTA. Yes, Karl, very much. Where did Franz go?

KARL. Oh, running around telling everyone his good fortune!

MARTA. What are you thinking?

KARL. Oh, those Americans—look how they dance. I wonder whether I could ever learn to dance like that.

MARTA. Neither you nor I, Karl. We were born on the wrong side of the Atlantic for that.

KARL. Why do you say that? You talk so much about becoming an American.

MARTA. I want to with all my heart, but there will always be this difference between us and them. They were born to freedom. To them it is like the air they breathe. They aren't even conscious of it. Freedom is of them and they are of freedom.

KARL (*bitterly*). Isn't it better for America to have people like *us* who *think* about freedom, who *worry* about it, who know what it means *not* to have it, and so know enough to want to *live* for it?

MARTA. In times like these, yes, but there will be other times when the fight is won, and it is of these times and of our child I am thinking. I want for him to be an American from his first cry. I want freedom to be in the first air he breathes for that cry. I want for him that in a world gone mad with the ravings of little men, he should be born in a country that remains sane and firm in its convictions that man as an individual has certain inalienable rights.

(*The music stops behind her above speech. Murmur of voices.*)

KARL. I love you, Marta.

FRANZ (*fade-in*). Look! Look who I brought back to join us!

MARTA. Why, Mr. Holst!

HOLST. Good evening, Madame Kroft. Mr. Kroft.

KARL. How do you do, Mr. Holst!

FRANZ. Well, let's all sit down! Waiter! Beer for everybody!

HOLST. And how are you, Mrs. Kroft?

MARTA. Is everything all right?

HOLST. Concerning your visit this afternoon?

MARTA. Yes.

HOLST. Oh, yes, yes, everything is going splendidly!

MARTA. Then I am still very happy.

FRANZ. Of course you are! We're all happy tonight!

(*The piano starts waltz again, continuing far back behind.*)

FRANZ. Come, Mrs. Kroft, you must dance with me. I—oh, I'm sorry, I forgot.

MARTA. And so did I—almost. Karli, you better take me home, now.

KARL. Yes, of course.

MARTA. Good night, Franz.

FRANZ. Good night.

MARTA. Good night, Mr. Holst. I'll be waiting so anxiously to hear from you.

HOLST. Believe me—you will.

KARL. Come, dear. Good night. (*Fade*) Good night.

MARTA (*fading with him*). Good night.

FRANZ. Ah, wonderful couple, eh, Mr. Holst?

HOLST (*flatly*). I want to talk about *you!* So tomorrow you leave us?

FRANZ. Yes, my waiting is at an end.

HOLST. As soon as you are in America, you will send for your family?

FRANZ. Why, yes. Of course.

HOLST. Then you have plenty of money to take care of them?

FRANZ. What are you trying to say?

HOLST. I'm not trying. I'm *saying* it! Franz Bruckner, you are to give me the money you stole from your country.

FRANZ. Stole? W-what are you talking about?

HOLST. The information came to me today! The money you took with you when you left Europe!

FRANZ. But it was my own money! Mine! I'd worked for it all my life! And what affair is it of *yours?*

HOLST. You are very fond of your wife and children, Bruckner?

FRANZ (*slowly, with effort*). What are you saying?

HOLST. I'm saying that if you're concerned for the future welfare of your wife and children, you will give me the money! At once!

FRANZ. You—you're bluffing! You can't do a thing to my family!

HOLST (*slowly, coldly, measuredly*). Must I wear a uniform to convince you? My name is Sigmund Holst—*Captain* Sigmund Holst!

FRANZ (*dazedly*). Secret police! That's why you're here. I didn't think—I . . .

HOLST. I have no more time to waste! The money?

FRANZ (*completely defeated*). You will have the money in the morning.

(*Musical transition.*)

MARTA (*softly*). Karl. . . .

KARL. Hmmmm?

MARTA. What time is it?

KARL. About midnight. Can't sleep?

MARTA. No.

KARL. Get you some water?

MARTA. No.

KARL. So hot. Moonlight so bright, isn't it?

MARTA. It's shining here—and in America.

KARL. Marta, darling, you said yourself tonight everything was all right!

MARTA. Karli, supposing he lied to us. . . .

KARL (*a little too abruptly*). Of course not! Mr. Holst wouldn't lie about a thing like this! What would be his object? He is a respectable merchant. He'd *have* to give us our money back!

MARTA. Put your arms around me—both. . . .

KARL (*soothingly*). It'll be all right. Must be . . .

(*Fade-in sound of disturbance down the street, shouts of men, etc.*)

KARL. That noise! What in the world . . . ?

MARTA. Some trouble down in the street!

KARL. No—don't try to get up. (*Fade*) I'll find out what it is.

(*Sounds in street rise.*)

MARTA. What is it?

KARL. I don't know! People running about—police . . .

MARTA. Karl, please find out!

KARL. Yes, I will!

(*Door opening, back.*)

KARL (*calling*). Desk clerk! Jose! You—there—come here!

VOICE (*fading-in*). Yes, señor? What is it, señor?

KARL. That noise out in the street, of course! What's going on out there?

VOICE. Oh, señor, *muchas* trouble, *sí, sí!*

MARTA (*fade-in*). Karl, what is it?

KARL. Marta! Marta, you shouldn't have left the bed.

MARTA. I'm all right! What's the trouble?

Voice. Oh, señora! *Muchas* trouble! Señor Bruckner!

Karl. Bruckner?

Marta. Franz! What about Franz?

Voice. He is shot!

(*Both* Karl *and* Marta *gasp.*)

Voice. *Sí,* shot dead, but first he killed Señor Holst.

Marta. Oh, no!

Karl. Jose! What are you saying?

Voice. The truth, señor! Señor Bruckner killed Señor Holst,
and then the police they shot Señor Bruckner! *Sí,* it is the
truth!

Karl. But why should Franz . . . ?

Marta. Boy, tell us! Why did Franz shoot Mr. Holst?

Voice. You do not know?

Karl. Know *what?*

Marta. What?

Voice. Señor Holst, he was one of those people from Europe
—*sí* . . . I think the word is Secret Police.

Marta. Karl! My baby! (*Sighs as she faints.*)

(*Thud of body on floor.*)

Karl. Marta! Jose! Get Dr. Caspar! Run! Oh, Marta!

Marta (*in close, in pain*). Dr. Caspar. . . .

Karl. Jose! Why do you stand there?

Jose. The doctor—he is gone!

(*Musical transition.*)

(*Sound of small truck moving along over rough road, down
and continuing back behind.*)

Jose (*calling*). Señor Kroft!

Karl (*back, muffled as if heard through cab of truck*). Yes?

Jose. Señor, maybe it is better we stop? She is so sick—
she . . .

Karl (*back*). She says to go on!

JOSE. Oh, señor, it is not good.

(*Sound of truck up as transition and fade far back behind.*)

MARTA (*throughout the following scene she is in spasmodic agony of childbirth*). Karl!

KARL. Yes, dear. . . .

MARTA. Don't let him—stop.

KARL. Oh, Marta, I tell you it would be wisest . . .

MARTA. I am not—asking for wisdom—just—to get over the border. . . .

KARL. I beg you—let me tell Jose to stop the truck. If not for your sake—the sake of the child.

MARTA (*not listening*). You said—if it was a girl—that was all right, too!

KARL. Marta, please! Listen to me! Jose took this truck from the hotel—he had no right! And we have no right to cross the border. We may never find the border—so dark—this is not even a road—a trail.

MARTA. West of the Rockies—he'll be a pioneer.

KARL. Marta, try to understand! It was madness to start! The hospital in Mexicali—we must turn back!

MARTA. No, no, no! If he's an American, he'll have something to live for! I won't let you stop the truck! Never, never, never!

KARL. But our quota number—it will come up sooner or later, and then we can live in America always, and we will become citizens, and then, no matter where the child is born, *he* will be a citizen!

MARTA. No! No! In America! He's got to be born an American! How many times must I say it? It's different when you're born an American. You start there, so it's yours! America has got to be my baby's!

KARL. Oh, Marta, how can you endure . . . ?

MARTA. I will! I will! They walk like gods, these Americans! And they are gods because they have freedom to think, and speak, and do what they want! And I will get that for my son. (*Pain is extreme*) I will! (*Her gasp as she faints*) Ahhhhh!

KARL. Jose! Jose! Stop! Stop the truck! Oh, Marta!

(*Truck coming to stop.*)

JOSE (*back*). What is it?

KARL. Come back here quickly! (*As he administers to* MARTA) Oh, Marta—I—I don't know what . . .

JOSE (*fade-in*). Señor! What . . . ?

KARL. Climb in here! Quick!

(*Sound of scramble.*)

JOSE. What's happen? Señora . . .

KARL. I—I don't know—fainted!

JOSE. Here—hold the lantern!

KARL (*weepily*). Oh, Marta!

(MARTA *moans.*)

JOSE. I think I know what to do—*si.* . . .

KARL (*moans*). Why did I ever listen to her?

JOSE. The lantern—over more!

KARL. Marta!

(*We hear cry of new-born child.*)

KARL. Jose! Is she . . . ?

JOSE. *Si—si*—she is all right. . . .

MARTA (*with effort*). Karl—did we stop?

KARL. Yes.

MARTA. Karl, I—I told you not . . .

JOSE. A son.

MARTA. Karl.

KARL. Marta—a son.

MARTA. But—he wasn't born on American . . . Karl (*Starts to weep weakly*) Oh, Karl. . . .

VOICE (*American—fading-in*). You! Come out of there!

KARL. Jose! Who . . . ?

JOSE. It is a *soldat*. . . .

VOICE (*in full*). Say, what's going on in there?

JOSE. Who are you?

VOICE. U. S. Border Patrol! What's going on here?

MARTA. Karl, what did he say?

VOICE. I said I'm with the U. S. Border Patrol! Say, what's the matter . . . ?

(*Cry of new-born child again.*)

VOICE (*seeing*) Gosh!

MARTA. Oh, Karl, did you hear? United States border . . . Karl. . . . Karl. . . .

KARL. Yes, *liebchen?*

MARTA. Put your head—close. . . .

KARL. Yes?

MARTA. Look (*Whispers*) An American is born. . . .

(*Musical curtain.*)

THE IMMORTAL GENTLEMAN

I looked at the crime and the criminals. Pages of the newspaper were filled with the record of their horrors, terrible misdeeds which, in some future history-book, might occupy but a few paragraphs in a chapter on "The Second Dark Age" —but to us here in the now these pages were wet with the blood and the tears.

And then, in the back pages of that same news sheet, I read solemn words of a conference of medical men meeting, in this time of mass murder, to discuss the scientific extension of man's life-span.

Knowing of these two mad juxtapositions, you will understand why The Immortal Gentleman *happened.*

THE IMMORTAL GENTLEMAN

(*Music up, then fade behind.*)

VOICE. Beautiful, that the hands of the sisters, Death and Night, incessantly, softly wash again and ever again, this soiled world.

(*Music up, then fade-out.*)

EARL (*chuckling*). Don't be frightened, Joan. Please, don't be! Yes, yes, I know I screamed, but don't be afraid for me! I'm all right, really I am!

JOAN. But, Earl . . .

EARL. No, no, don't say anything—just listen! The reason that I screamed . . . It made me happy . . . I—oh, I know it sounds confused, but I can talk to you freely now, for the first time since I've known you! (*Seriously*) Joan, I want to tell you about it now, talk it out completely, tell you about myself and then you'll understand and then we'll both be happy! Remember you once said that you never *could* be happy with me? I knew why. You thought I was a coward!

JOAN. Earl . . .

EARL. No, don't answer; if you speak I'll want to hold you in my arms. (*Determinedly*) And I've got to talk this thing out first! Talk it out from the time before I knew you until a few moments ago when I screamed and frightened you. You were right. I have been a coward, but not about men or things or living—just of—*not* living. I can see in your eyes that you don't know what I mean. Must I say it? Must I say the word? All right I will! I've been afraid of—death.

A victory for me even to *say* the word. Yes, Joan, as long as I can remember, death has been close to me, and so I've been afraid. I used to think of Him, I didn't give Him a name, standing at my shoulder waiting to cut off my breath, to shut off my sight, to take away all that I've wanted to see and do, and give me nothing, nothing in exchange! (*Down*) Yes, believe me, Joan, all my life it was that way. Even as a boy, I couldn't be happy because of— *that!* Light in the sky and I wanted to see it forever! Dark in the night and I wanted to know it forever. So two thoughts were in me all through life: if I could only live forever—if I wouldn't die—if I could only live forever— if I wouldn't die—if I'd only live forever . . . The two thoughts chasing each other in a mad, never-ending circle! Not to die—to live forever—not to die—to live forever— over and over and over. So there was no happiness in me, and much as I loved you, I could give you no happiness, and the fear in me was in my face and in my work and you knew it and everyone knew it, but they didn't know why *you* said and *they* said "Poor cowardly Earl! Unfortunate man, he cannot face life!" But what I couldn't face was—*death!*

(*Man's voice crying out far, far back echo chamber.*)

EARL. So tonight I cried out in fear in front of everyone—the echo of it's still in my ears. And I'm going to tell you why I cried out, then you'll understand me and why I say I'm free and happy for the first time in my life. And, Joan, if it's too strange to believe, just listen patiently. We were sitting in the auditorium, you and I—the politician up on the stage, talking—talking. . . .

SPEAKER (*fade-in, echo slight*). . . . and in this coming election, I repeat again, the issue will be clear—an issue made clear by our glorious party! You young men and women of this community, it is your duty to awaken to the full duty of your citizenship! (*Fade*) It is your duty at this coming election to do more than come out to the polls. You must discuss these issues with your friends at your bridge parties and clubs . . . (*Fade far, far back, continuing behind.*)

EARL (*stream of consciousness, monotone*). Sitting there—you next to me—I wasn't listening to him on the stage. I was thinking the same infernal thoughts I'd thought all my life whenever I was alone, Of Him! Him! And then:

LEADER (*fade-in slowly, crisply*). So I say to all of you assembled here that it is a challenge to youth—yes, to youth—to everyone of you here . . . (*Fade*) A challenge that we must accept, face, and challenge in turn, for this, indeed, is an issue that is so close to each of us that not to discuss it bravely and act bravely is to put an end to all that we hold near and dear. (*Continue far back ad lib. Words are unintelligible.*)

EARL (*on cue*). Speaker's voice wasn't the same. I looked up. No, not the same! The other one an old man—this one young—couldn't quite see his face! So dark in the hall! Had something happened to the lights? I turned toward you, said, (*Straight*) "Joan, when did the lights . . ." I stopped! You weren't there! Believe me—not there! Another woman!

GEYNA. Did you speak to me?

EARL. She said that! I said, (*Straight*) "Where—where is Joan?"

GEYNA. Joan? Who is Joan?

EARL. She was sitting right next to me! She . . .

GEYNA. Shh!

EARL (*down*). You have her chair. Where did she . . . ? I

mean the young lady who was sitting here—where did she go?

GEYNA. I've been here for hours.

EARL. But she was here—here, I tell you. . . .

GEYNA. Quiet! Quiet! The speaker—listen!

LEADER (*ad lib slightly for a few seconds, then back and far behind*). The time has passed for pleadings! The time is passed for petitions! We are representative of youth, and youth is the time for action. So we must act! Yes, act! (*Ad lib as before until cue.*)

EARL. The speaker—what did he matter? I sat there. Couldn't figure it out. You, Joan—where had you gone? Could I have dozed off, and you slipped out, and this other woman taken your place? Yet, how strange your leaving without a word! And then: (*Wind sighs softly*) Wind! Wind in the auditorium? I looked up. (*Gasp*) The sky! No roof! A single star and clouds! (*Puzzled*) No roof! Sleep? No, awake! I got up to go . . .

GEYNA (*whispering*). No, no! Sit down! No one can leave!

EARL (*whispering*). But, my friend . . .

GEYNA. You have sworn to stay! You must!

EARL (*puzzled*). I sat down! Sworn to stay! What in the world . . . ? I sat down.

LEADER (*fade-in fast*). There can be no compromise! There will be no compromise! For, if we compromise, we are doomed as they have always doomed us. (*Fade and continue ad lib as before.*)

EARL. Speaker—what did he matter! No roof on the place. Crazy! How could a roof disappear in a moment without . . . I said to the girl: (*Whispering*) "Where is the roof? What's happened to this place? Where are we?"

GEYNA (*whispers*). You know!

EARL. Know? Know what? I'd get out of the place! I'd find you, Joan! Started to go again! The girl's hand tight on my wrist!

GEYNA (*whispering*). No, don't. You swore to stay.

EARL. Swore?

GEYNA. *You* swore! *They* swore! He speaks the truth!

EARL. But what . . . ?

GEYNA. Listen! *Listen!*

LEADER (*fade-in fast*). And now, good friends, let us put an end to words. This meeting of ours was destined—for five hundred years—destined!

EARL (*in close, stream of consciousness*). What was he saying? For five hundred years destined? For what?

LEADER. None of us can say we have moved quickly, for in the meditation of these five hundred years has come the essence of truth, a truth that burns bright in the hearts of all of us.

EARL. What kind of political speech was that?

LEADER. And so an end to words! In this meeting we have spoken words which none dare question! Now the time has come for action, which none dare deny us!

EARL. The girl leaned close and whispered:

GEYNA (*in close, whispering*). None dare deny us!

EARL. Deny us? *Deny* what? Wanted to yell out just the way I did a few moments ago, but I couldn't! Something about the place—the speaker—people around me . . . I could only sit there, questions pounding in my head . . .

LEADER (*in fast*). Youth is action! Action is youth! We will act together and make ourselves a new world—a better world! Our world!

(*Murmur of voices as meeting breaks up, down behind.*)

EARL. Meeting over—everyone getting up. The girl said:

GEYNA. Come with me!

EARL. Where?

GEYNA. You know.

EARL. I know!

(*Murmur of crowd.*)

EARL (*puzzled*). Crowd pressing around me—dark, strange faces—young, angry faces—none of my friends. My friends —where were they? Joan, where were you? The auditorium in ruins—as she led me out I saw that! It *was* madness! Yet a strangely intriguing madness . . . So I walked with her. (*Sound of door*) Led me through a door . . . (*Murmur of voices back*) I could hear voices. She said:

(*Fade voices far back.*)

GEYNA (*whispering*). Stand here a moment. I want to talk to you. Tell me—why do you act so strangely? Don't you want to go through with it?

EARL. Through with what?

GEYNA. There! That is what I mean! You talk as if you don't *know!*

EARL. I couldn't speak. Stood there . . .

GEYNA. It's a glorious morning for all of us! We've waited five hundred years, some of us, for this!

EARL. Five hundred years? What was she . . . ? I said: "Five hundred years?"

GEYNA. Well, perhaps not you. But *I've* waited three hundred fifty myself!

EARL (*blankly*). W-what did you say?

GEYNA. Three hundred and fifty years, and now I can't wait another moment! The thought of another empty day suffocates me!

EARL (*slowly*). Am I insane—or you?

GEYNA. Insane? I don't know the word.

EARL (*sharply*). Out of your head! You or I?

GEYNA. Yo*u* *are* a strange one! And yet you came here! Why?

EARL. To hear a speech!

GEYNA. So! To hear—but not to act, eh? You will! You will! (*Fade*) All of us will!

EARL. And then—the moonlight from under a cloud and then her face. I saw her face clearly for the first time. Hers was a loveliness beyond the word. Sixteen—seventeen—she couldn't have been more—freshness of the morning. And yet her eyes—old, bright, wise. So strange—her old eyes in that young face. I—I stood there—staring at her.

GEYNA (*in fast*). I tell you this: If one of us fails, we all fail—and that can't happen! Remember that! Now come! (*Fade*) They're waiting!

(*Fade-in voices.*)

EARL. Followed her . . . A room—quite dark—many people in it . . .

(*Fade-in murmur of small group of people, hold behind.*)

LEADER (*off slightly*). Quiet, please! Quiet! (*Murmur out, in full*) There is little time to waste! We will now draw lots. Each of you take a slip as the box is passed. Most of the slips are blank; only twenty-four are numbered. Whoever draws a numbered slip stays. The others go.

(*Murmur up, then fade.*)

EARL. Slips—draw lots . . . What was this? Draw lots for what? Someone came close and held out a box. The girl said:

GEYNA. Take a paper!

EARL. I did—she did—the others did. The girl said:

GEYNA. Look at the slip.

EARL. I did. A number—eleven. She said:

GEYNA. Good! I too!

EARL. Held out the paper in her hand . . . I saw the number twelve on it.

GEYNA. You and I! You and I!

EARL. She and I *what?* The Leader spoke again:

LEADER (*fade-in*). All those without numbers leave! (*Fade*) All those without numbers leave!

(*Murmur of voices fade-in behind.*)

EARL. The push of bodies around me, (*Voices out*) and in a moment there were only a few left. The girl at my side motionless, until the Leader said:

LEADER: Now we can risk lights.

EARL. In a moment lights began to glow. I stood there blinking and then—I saw! (*Slowly*) Twenty-four people in that room, men and women; twenty-four—I counted them—and *all of them looked alike!* Yes, alike, I tell you! Men and women—but their faces as the girl's. Twenty-four faces alike as copies of a picture strung along a wall! They, in turn, were staring at me. . . .

VOICE No. 1. Who is he?

EARL. A voice said.

VOICE No. 2. Who is he?

EARL. Another said.

(*Murmur of voices.*)

EARL. They came close around me . . .

VOICES. Not one of us. Who is he? Who is he? Not one of us . . .

EARL. All those faces—alike—staring—talking—staring—talking . . .

(*Murmur of voices up slightly, then fade behind.*)

EARL. The girl spoke. I knew it was she because her hand had been on my arm.

174

GEYNA. Leave him alone! He is an atavar!

VOICES (*murmur, fade slowly*). Atavar! An atavar! Oh! An atavar! Atavar!

EARL. Atavar! What was an atavar? I—I wanted to speak but she spoke.

GEYNA (*in fast*). He'll be all right. I'll see to that.

LEADER. But an atavar! Unpredictable!

GEYNA. But I tell you he'll be with me! He drew eleven—I drew twelve! (*Fade*) He'll be with me!

LEADER (*back*). But they're undependable! You know that! (*Fade far back*) Never can tell about an atavar!

GEYNA (*far, far back, arguing*). But I'll take care of him! (*Continues to argue ad lib, far, far back behind.*)

EARL. They stood there arguing about me, Joan. Yes, arguing about *me!* Whether I could . . . Whether I would . . . Whether I was reliable—unreliable . . . And always that word atavar, atavar, atavar! Mad dreams or mad adventure, whatever it was, I didn't know. (*Stop argument*) Their argument stopped.

(*Ad lib out abruptly.*)

EARL. Apparently the girl had won. The Leader said:

LEADER (*fade-in*). All right, atavar, you'll be with her! (*Up*) Now, all of you listen! This atavar is with us, and with us he'll stay until it's ended.

EARL (*quickly, intensely*). Ended? Ended? What had begun and what would end?

LEADER (*fade-in*). One question, atavar—what is your age?

EARL. My age? You want to know my age?

LEADER. Didn't you hear, atavar? What is your age?

EARL. The girl said:

GEYNA (*whispering*). Tell him!

EARL. My—my age is twenty-five.

LEADER (*after pause, blankly*). What did you say?

EARL. Twenty-five.

GEYNA (*whispering*). Do not joke! Tell us your age!

EARL. I told you! Twenty-five! For a moment, no one spoke. They looked at each other—shook their heads slowly— shoulders shrugged . . .

VOICE No. 2 (*whispers*). An atavar! Just an atavar!

EARL. She said:

GEYNA. Don't worry, any of you. I'll take care of him. He'll do as he's told. . . .

EARL. Do as I was told? Do what? Told to do what? I opened my mouth to speak, and then I didn't, because the Leader said:

LEADER (*fade-in*). All right! Our last word! There are twenty-four of you—twelve pairs! Each pair will go out together! If one fails, the other will succeed!

VOICE No. 1 (*off*). But when . . . ?

LEADER. Now! At once! We have waited long enough for *them!* I alone have waited four hundred years.

VOICE No. 2. And I, two hundred!

VOICE No. 1. And I, three hundred!

VOICE No. 3. I, four hundred and twenty-five!

VOICES (*fading*). Two hundred and thirty! A hundred and seventy-five! Three hundred and sixty! (*Etc., far back behind.*)

EARL. I understood! Like a blow on the head, I understood. These people—mad! Yes, that was it! Talking of living hundreds of years—out of their heads all of them! Listening to them, I knew that!

VOICES (*fade-in*). Three hundred and forty years! I waited four hundred and seventy years! (*Fade back, continue ad lib as before.*)

EARL. And that explained the likeness of their faces! Some sort of weird inter-breeding of a family resulting in feeble-mindedness! How did I come among them? (*Ad lib fades out, wind sighs softly*) Went outside—the girl with me . . . Everyone going off in pairs, their faces tense and angry . . . Going off to some strange madness. The girl said:

GEYNA. Wait here! I'll get what we need, then we'll keep our appointment. (*Fade*) Wait here!

EARL. Joan, believe me, as she went off into the darkness leaving me there alone, I swear my head was spinning as if it were on a pivot, as it spun the thoughts in my head spun with it!

(*Whine of spinning top behind.*)

VOICES (*full, fading on cue*).

Madness!

Dream!

MADNESS!

DREAM!

MADNESS!

DREAM!

(*Continuing until cue.*)

EARL. What was happening to me? And then a thought: Had what I feared all my life happened at last? Had I (*Voices cut cold*) died?

VOICES. Dead! Dead! Dead! Dead!

(*Wind sighs.*)

EARL (*through chant of voices*). Joan, I remember the wind suddenly was cold about me, but I was colder. . . . (*Voices stop*) Dead? Was I . . . ? And then someone was standing by me. Not the girl but a man. Smooth, young, handsome face with those old, wise eyes looking at me. He said:

AHRO (*fade-in*). You have not started yet, atavar!

EARL. No—no. . . .

AHRO. Strange. I have never seen you before. There are so few atavars. You know, generally, they are not permitted to develop.

EARL. Looking at him, I knew I was alive! Of course! And dream! This was no dream!

AHRO. Yes, there are so few atavars.

EARL. I said: "Atavars? Atavars? What in the devil are atavars?"

AHRO. You are a strange one!

EARL. Tell me! What are atavars? Why call me an atavar?

AHRO. Because you are. You are not like us, you know. You are a throwback to the individualistic, unconditioned, embryonic development.

EARL (*blankly*). Wha-at?

AHRO (*laughs softly*). But then, of course, you don't understand, do you? No, an atavar wouldn't.

EARL. Tell me!

AHRO. It is strange they should have permitted you to develop and not have explained to you the difference.

EARL. What difference? What?

AHRO. Once in every two thousand births—and that means once in every two thousand years—we don't have many new ones in the world, you know—something happens in the incubation process and, instead of one of us perfected ones, one of *you* develops. A throwback to ancient times, an imperfect creature of the past. In other words an atavism. (*Fade*) Understand? An atavism.

EARL (*stream of consciousness*). Atavism—atavar—atavism— what in the devil's name was this? But he kept talking! He said:

AHRO. Yet, atavar though you are, life must be miserable for you as it is for the rest of us.

EARL. Life—miserable . . .

AHRO. Well, of course! Why else would you have joined with us? Oh, this is going to be a glorious night for us! (*Bitterly*) But not for *them!*

EARL (*confusedly*). I—I don't understand exactly what . . .

AHRO (*laughs softly*). Of course not! Things *would* be confused for the atavar mind, wouldn't they? That's the infernal trouble with *our* minds. Things are much too clear and concise and understandable! They bred all the confusion out of us a long time ago! Well, now they'll pay for it!

EARL. Please—tell me.

AHRO. Just look at *me!* I've lived just a handful of years—two hundred and fifty . . .

EARL (*stream of consciousness*). He said that, Joan! Yes, believe me! Two hundred and fifty years!

AHRO (*fade-in fast*). And yet, believe me, atavar, I'm weary unto the death we'll never know!

EARL (*repeats softly, slowly*). Death—we'll never know!

AHRO. What good is there in it for any of us living forever?

EARL (*repeats softly, slowly*). Living—forever!

AHRO. For the first fifty years of our lives they condition us—all right! We come out with our brains filled with all knowledge of all time! Paragons all! Geniuses all! But what good does it do us? What good? Always *they* are in the way!

EARL. They?

AHRO (*wearily*). Look, atavar, you can't be so completely a fool, or they would never have let you out! *They* are the old ones, and what is interesting and exciting in the world they do! They, no one else! And we, who came after them, after they conditioned the world against sickness, illness, age and death—we have nothing left to do! They hold the key positions, they, and we stand by and grind the weary years away in nothingness! A world of youth, of the want to do, and there is nothing to do! And yet there are worlds out there where we might go, but again they stand in our way and say no, it shouldn't be done! They, they the old ones all around us holding us down, giving us everlasting life, and then giving us nothing to live for! But this night will change it. You and I and the rest of us twenty-four! Well, here comes your partner. I must go to mine! (*Fade*) Good-bye, atavar, good luck!

(*Wind sighs, fading out.*)

EARL. He was gone, and then the girl at my side. Under her arm a small black box.

GEYNA. All right, we can go now. . . .

EARL. She took my arm; we walked along. In almost a moment we were in a straight, broad street—straight and shiny and glistening, bright with a light I've never seen. A quiet, empty street—clean and bright and strange—as if in a dream. A dream! (*Angrily*) This was no dream! And then she said:

GEYNA. In here!

EARL. We stepped on a platform—part of the sidewalk, and it was moving, carrying us swiftly, swiftly down the street! (*Sound of rush of air down far behind*) An escalator— moving sidewalk—I don't know what! Faster, faster— things rushing by—strange towering buildings—and parks, and always that light—strange light. And then I heard that she was talking to me.

(*Air in a little, then down.*)

180

GEYNA (*fade-in*). I saw you talking to Ahro. He has the easy one. We've a hard one.

EARL. Two hundred and fifty years, he said. . . .

GEYNA. Ahro? Yes, that's true.

EARL. Lived two hundred and fifty years?

GEYNA. It isn't much, I know—you must be older! Or are you? Hard to tell with an atavar.

EARL (*slowly*). How—old—are you?

GEYNA. I? Four hundred! Four hundred years—but not of living!

EARL. What—what do you mean?

GEYNA. You know! *They,* with all their years! Before we were born, they took the work of the world, and what is left for us? To wander up and down—pretty ornaments with empty lives! But they forgot one thing! They left ambition in us, and this night we'll find a place to use it!

EARL. How?

GEYNA. Atavar, you *are* a fool! You *know,* and yet you *don't* know! How can we find a place for ourselves as long as *they* do as they please? Listen—in the very ancient world, men lived a few years and then died, and they thought that was horrible; but that was good! For, when they died, there was a place for youth! Yes, one would fall, and a young one took his place. Sometimes he did better than the one who had gone before, so the world progressed. But now, no one falls, no one dies, and so the old ones stay and stay and stay and we, the young ones, have no place, and when we want to make a place the old ones say "No!"

(*Rush of air up as transition, then back behind.*)

EARL. The thing we were riding climbed higher; higher spirals inclined up along the side of a huge glistening build-

ing that glittered in that light! Higher! Higher! And still
she talked!

(*Air up slightly, then back behind.*)

GEYNA. We've pleaded and petitioned and they do not listen,
so tonight we act. You and I, atavar, one of twenty-four!

EARL. Act? What do you . . . ?

GEYNA. By turning back the time to when men died and gave
the younger ones their place!

EARL (*gasp*). What?

GEYNA. The wrong of each man died with him when he died
in that old world; and so tonight we'll see that wrongs are
given their belated rest!

EARL. How? *How?* (*Rush of air up as transition, then back
behind*) Higher—higher—the moving staircase taking us
higher every second along a building stretching up into in-
finity! Higher, higher the wind singing in my ears! (*Rush
of wind fading-in*) And still she talked!

(*Rush of air up, then down behind.*)

GEYNA (*laughs*). You and I, atavar, we'll do our part—up
there!

(*Rush of wind up, then down behind.*)

EARL. She was pointing up. I looked up to where the building
ended in the clouds!

(*Wind up, then back behind.*)

GEYNA. *She* sits up there. Five thousand years she's lived—
every day since the day Science shut out death! Five thousand years, but tonight *we* begin to live! *Here!*

(*Wind up slightly.*)

EARL. Into my hand she thrust the black container! I said:
(*Up*) "What?"

GEYNA. You'll do it! *You!* In a moment we reach the spire!
She'll come out all smiles and happiness. They can be

happy, the old ones who have the work! Do it then! You must!

EARL. What?

GEYNA. Throw it at her, and she'll be free of life, and we will be free of life without living! You'll do it, atavar! You will! Throw it at her!

(*Wind up, then down behind.*)

EARL. Throw it! What? The thing in my hands? What did she mean—to free that person up there from life? The weight in my hands! Then, suddenly, I realized! Some kind of explosive . . . She expected me to throw it at that person up in the tower! Me, to kill!

(*Wind up, then down.*)

GEYNA. You will! You will!

EARL. No! *No!* The word tore through my head, and with it tore away confusion! I *knew!* I *understood!* This was the world of the future, where science had doomed the death I feared! Men lived forever and these young ones had no chance! And now they were out to kill and make their chance! And I was to kill *for* them, *with* them!

(*Escalator up again, then down.*)

GEYNA. You will! You will! You will! (*Continuing back behind.*)

EARL. No! I won't! Not my world! Not mine! I want to go back! Stop saying that! I won't!

GEYNA (*up intensely*). There she is! The matriarch! Throw it! Throw it!

EARL. I won't kill! Not I! I won't! She began to struggle with me for the explosive!

GEYNA (*back, struggling*). Give it to me! Give me that! Give me!

EARL. I cried out, "No!" I jumped!

(*Music and rush of wind building behind.*)

EARL. Falling! I was falling! Through the horrible space of that horrible future. Down and down and down. The glistening sides of the building rushing past me! Down, twisting, clawing at the air. Down and down. And then I remembered. In my arms. That explosive. I tried to throw it. But my hands were tight around it. I couldn't unlock them. The ground coming up. I screamed.

(*Music and wind out knife-clean.*)

EARL (*down*). And there I was—sitting next to you in the hall where I had been before. The politician up on the stage—my friends around me—you next to me, frightened at my cry . . . Yes, and the roof quite intact above me. . . . (*Sighs deeply*) So here it ends, Joan. Sitting there, I stepped ahead in time into a day when men had conquered death. And so, somehow, I—I'm not afraid of Him any more, the one at my shoulder, because I think it's good that men should live, then die, and so end the evil in them and give their place to others. Joan, tell me—don't you agree?

(*Music down behind.*)

VOICE. Beautiful, that the hands of the sisters, Death and Night, incessantly, softly wash again and ever again, this soiled world.

(*Musical curtain.*)

THESE ARE YOUR BROTHERS

Christmas.

Write us something covered with tinsel and singing with the happiness of children and the joyous ringing of bells on a frosty morning.

No! *Write us something covered with the blood of this Christmas! Tune the words to the shriek of a woman being strafed by a Stuka which has centered on her as a military objective! Rhyme the words to the goose-stepping of a firing squad leading out the hostages of the "New Order!"*

But all I could write was These Are Your Brothers.

THESE ARE YOUR BROTHERS

(*Fade-in sound of Christmas crowds in metropolitan district, down after few seconds, continuing back behind.*)

JOE (*he is a street-corner Santa Claus; one of Broadway's wise guys, as cynical as a disappointed lover; these words are stream of consciousness*). Seven o'clock . . . Three more hours, he said . . . Yeah! Half an hour more and I scram . . . Uh—suit's hot—suit . . . I wonder how much Abe'll give me for it. Five bucks! Sure, Santa Claus suit oughtta be worth a fin. . . . So I'll take three . . . Clear profit . . . Old Droop-face'll be waitin' for me to turn in the outfit. . . . Will *he* wait! Yeah! Street's pretty crowded . . . Maybe I'd better start ringin' the bell. Saps might throw a couple o' nickels . . . Yeah, night before Christmas . . . Plenty o' saps . . .

(*Sound of ringing small hand-bell, fade back after few seconds, continuing far back behind.*)

JOE. What a racket! Rent Santa suit two bucks, and make a sawbuck a day! Come on, you umpchays—give!

(*Sound of coins in tin cup.*)

JOE (*up*). Thank ya, ma'am, thank ya! Merry Christmas! (*Down, stream of consciousness*) How much did the broad . . . ? (*Disgustedly*) Nickel! Oh, well, it's a beer. . . . (*Bell ringing starts again*) Look at 'em hurryin' . . . Chumps! All of 'em, chumps . . . Wear a red suit and chin whiskers and wave a tin cup at 'em, and they give! Chumps! All of 'em, chumps! (*Sound of coins in cup, bell out*) Thank you, sir. A Merry Christmas to you! (*Ringing*

187

again) Two bits! Nice goin'! Merry Christmas, chump, two bits worth . . . Yeah, chumps, all of 'em. Everybody's a chump! Peace on earth, good will to who? Come on, chumps—give! Everybody's takin' a slug at everybody else, and everybody's got his knife out for everybody else, and it's dog eat dog, and this is one guy that knows it. Everybody out to get everything they can lay their hands on, from the top-hat guys down to the lugs they're kickin' around. Dog eat dog and (*Board fade*) get all you can get and to the devil with the other guy. Just dog eat dog—dog eat dog . . .

(*Two-beat transitional pause. Board fade-in harp strains, segue into factory whistle blowing. Murmur of men's voices coming off shift from steel mill. Record backing up ad libs.*)

VOICES (*Croatians, Poles, Negroes*).

Hey, Hasan, I give you lift home!

How much overtime you make this week, Nick?

Me, I don' buy presents for nobody but the kids this year—nobody!

Hey, you t'ink we get full time after Christmas?

(*Fade*) I hear foreman say gonna mebbe shut down three plants till first of year!

Sonamagun, I feel good! For three days I don' do nothin' but eat and sleep! Betcha life! (*Fade.*)

Christmas, she's good for sleep and eat, but mostly for sleep, you betcha life. . . . Hey, Sam, you gonna work another shift tonight? Mr. Jackson, he say time and a half anybody work fixin' up new smelter!

SAM (*laughs*). Hey, you t'ink Ah'm crazy? You t'ink Ah'm goin' spen' mah Chris'mus day 'round old steel mill when Ah kin be sleepin' and eatin' and havin' mah fun?

STEVE. Sure, but time and a half!

SAM. Ain't no time and half fo' Sam on Chris'mus, big boy!
Whew, Ah sho' am tired!

STEVE. Me, too, but I go over to Nick's and get a couple drinks
in me, and then I start new shift! Me, I'm gonna make all
the time I can make, betcha life!

SAM. Okay, boy, okay, but not Sam, no, suh! Mah old money
pocket says go on workin', Sam, but mah back sho' talks
different! Home and bed's where Ah'm goin', yes, suh!

STEVE. Go on, you don't go home, not a big young fella like
you!

SAM (*chuckles*). Boy, da's smart talkin'!

STEVE (*laughs*). Sure, if I ain't for married and got t'ree kids
I go withya, betcha life!

SAM (*chuckles*). Not wheah Ah'm goin', big boy! Mah gal
she don' pay no nevah min' to nobody but Sam, 'specially
when it's de night befo' Chris'mus and ole Sam's handin'
out . . . Well, get on ole coat an' Ah'm high-tailin' out o'
heah, yes, suh!

STEVE. Aw, no! You come to Nick's, I buy you beer! Come
on!

SAM. No, suh! Ah'm sick ole steel town, man! What Ah
gotta do's git home, wash up, an' put on mah fancy suit!
Dat gal's waitin', mistuh!

STEVE (*fading*). Aw, come on!

SAM. No, suh, boy, heah I go! Take short cut over the ole
slag dump and git home and git goin', da's me!

STEVE (*far back*). Okay, Merry Christmas, Sam! Have good
time!

SAM. You betcha! Merry Chris'mus to you, too, big boy!
(*Door, wind, continuing behind. All his following speeches
are sotto until he reaches watchman*) Whee! Dat wind don'
like me! (*Chuckles*) Okay, wind, I don' lak you. Come on,

legs, pick 'em up and lay 'em down. Sam sho' want to git home, yes, suh! Pick 'em up and lay 'em down . . . (*Chuckles softly*) You gonna lak what I bring you, gal? You bettah lak it, suah put in lotsa time makin' de dough, yes, suh. . . . (*Wind howls*) Go 'way from me, wind . . . Ah'm tired. Work eighteen hours, dat's a long time for one man to throw dat shovel, yes, suh! Long time. . . . (*Wind howls*) Don' go pushin' me back, wind, I want to git home. . . . Yes, suh, dat gal . . . Ah got dat comin' to me, wind. Man work foh his fun, got it comin'! Hooey, Ah'm cold! Ole fingers dey break off. . . . Colder all de time . . . Gotta warm up! Ole watchman's shack—yeah—warm up in deah! (*Wooden door opening and closing, wind far, far back*) Evenin', mistuh! Min' if Ah warm mahself by yo' stove a couple minutes? Dat wind caught me crossin' de yard and jes' 'bout froze mah bones!

ED (*he is in his fifties and one of the defeated*). You work in the mill?

SAM. Dat's right! Numbah three Bessemer. What you do heah, mistuh? You watchman?

ED (*flatly*). Yeah. . . .

SAM. Mm, dat fire sho' do me good!

ED. I used to work in the mill and make good money. . . .

SAM. Why don' you work there now, mistuh? You ain't so ole!

ED. I got hurt—ten years ago—they gave me this. . . .

SAM. Well, dat's easy 'nuf sittin' in heah in de warm!

ED. Every hour I got to go out.

SAM. Wha' for?

ED. Walk down to the end of the fence, see everything's all right, turn a key, signal rings up in the main office, and then they know everything's okay. . . . Every hour I got to do that.

SAM (*chuckles*). Well, dat ain't so hard either, mistuh! Whammin' dat ole shovel, now dat's something. Jest walkin' and turnin' ole key, dat's sho' 'nuff easy!

ED (*repeats slowly*). Easy—no—not easy—not tonight. . . .

SAM. What yo' mean, not tonight?

ED. Why should I tell you?

SAM. Don' have to, mistuh, don' have to! Sam don' want to know nothin' but gittin' warm and finishin' crossin' de slag pile and gittin' hisself home!

ED. I sit here—I think, "If I only had somebody to talk to!"

SAM. Well, do yo' talkin' now, mistuh! Ah won' be heah long! Spit it right out, mistuh, and mebbe Ah won' even heah you!

ED. I get hurt in the plant. They give me this job—seven nights a week. I don't make much. Okay, it's a job. All night long—what's the difference if it's night?—make a livin'. What more does a man want? Make a livin'—all right. Every night, what's the difference? But not tonight . . . (*Tensely*) You gotta kid, black boy?

SAM. Kid? Me? (*Guffaws*) Naw!

ED. I gotta kid. Five years. Can you beat it? Old buck like me with a kid like that! Yeah, five years. You see, black boy, with a kid five years—every night it don't make a difference—but not tonight!

SAM. What yo' mean?

ED. He was born tonight—yeah, five years ago.

SAM. Sho' 'nuff?

ED. Yeah, why should I bull you? Five years tonight. That's somethin' for a man to think about, ain't it? Five years ago tonight. At night, and I work at night, so I never gets to see the kid. Never, I tell you. He ain't strong. When I get home he's still sleepin', and while I'm sleepin' he's up and out, so I never get to see the kid, I tell you! That don't make no difference. A man's gotta make a livin'—but not tonight, you understand me—not tonight! I gotta right to be with my kid on the day he was born! Yeah, fix up a tree and wake up in the mornin' and see him come runnin', playin' with the stuff I get him and maybe take him out on the sled in the mornin' and be with him like a guy should be with his kid! I gotta right to be with my kid tonight, black boy—I gotta right! (*For a second or two all that is heard is the soft whistle of the wind. He takes a deep shuddering breath, then:*) Huh! I guess it don't do me no good to have nobody stop in here. I'm alone so much, when I get started I shoot off my mouth. . . . Okay, black boy, you'll be moving on now. . . .

SAM (*flatly*). You . . .

ED. Huh!

SAM. You move, mistuh—not me.

ED (*tensely*). What're you talkin' 'bout?

SAM. Ah'm talkin' 'Merican, mistuh. Ah says, *you* go—*Ah'll* stay.

ED (*blankly*). Stay?

SAM (*impatiently*). Yeah, cain't you heah me? Stay—*stay!* Go on home to yo' kid. Ah'll stay heah! Go on home!

ED. You crazy?

SAM. Sho' Ah'm crazy! Crazy in de head! But how many times I got to tell you Ah'll stay!

ED. But—but . . .

SAM. Don' stand dere! Yo' want to be with dat kid? **Well**, *be* with him! It don' make no nevah min' to me. It don' make no nevah min' to nobody. Yo' show me where to turn dat thing to throw dat signal, and it don' make no nevah min' to de front office! Go on—go on, white man! Go home to yo' kid! Ah ain't tired. Ah ain't nothin'! Go on home to yo' kid, white man! Sam ain't got nothin' to do! (*Slowly*) Naw . . . Sam ain't got nothin' to do!

(*Music: harp strains at "Go on—go on" in above.*)

(*Board fade slowly. Fade-in traffic sounds and ringing of Santa Claus bell, down and continuing behind.*)

JOE. Come on, give, you chumps, give! What do you think I'm standin' here for? For my health? Give, you fat-faced, fat-headed, fat-bellied chumps! It's the night before Christmas! Give! It's dog eat dog, and tonight I'm doin' the eatin'! It's all phony. I'm a phony. Everybody's a phony, so come on, give! (*Up*) Thank you, ma'am. Merry Christmas. (*Down again, sotto*) A jitney for a phony. Phony Santa Claus—phony Christmas. You're a phony, lady! Everybody's a phony. World's all phonies. See me wavin' this phony flag at you, mister? "Peace on earth good will to men." That's the biggest phony, ain't it? "Peace on earth—yeah—good will to men—yeah . . . (*Fade*) Peace on earth, good will to men!

(*Board fade-in harp strains—music segue into splash of water, etc. Scene of battle cruiser in heavy sea, down and continuing behind.*)

OFFICER. The sea's getting heavier, eh, Harkins?

SAILOR. Aye, sir.

OFFICER. Well, I for one don't think we'll have trouble tonight. With that moon under and the wind freshening, a sub couldn't see us, unless . . .

VOICE (*back*). Submarine on the starboard bow!

(*Shouts of men . . . clanging of alarm bells.*)

Voice (*back*). Bearing—zero eight three! Range—five thousand yards!

Voice (*back*). Commence firing!

(*Heavy beat of one gun going off, followed by another, followed by rat-tat-tat of rapid-fire gun.*)

Voice (*in close, in quick alarm*). Look! On the starboard beam! Torpedo!

Voice. It's going to hit!

(*Tremendous reverberating explosion. Reverberating and fading slowly. Segue into water sound of man swimming, down and continuing behind.*)

Officer (*he has been blown off the deck of the cruiser and is now swimming in the darkness. These are the thoughts in his mind as he tries to keep afloat*). Afloat—got to keep afloat . . . (*Calls*) Help! Help! I'm in the water! Help! (*Down, stream of consciousness*) No . . . Save my breath . . . Sea's too high . . . Never hear me . . . Got to keep afloat until—until something happens . . . Find me . . . Keep afloat . . . Water cold . . . Swim—got to swim . . . (*For a few seconds we hear nothing but the water, then:*) Is everybody dead? Did the ship go under? I the only one left? (*Calls*) Help! Help me! (*Begins to cough as he swallows mouthful of water, then:*) Salt in my mouth . . . Afloat—try to keep afloat . . . So tired . . . Close my eyes and—no! Live! Got to live! Swim—got to live—got to live . . . Cynthia—got to live—no—can't swim any more . . . Going to die—die . . . I'll never . . . (*As his hand strikes something in the water*) Ah! Something! Hold on! (*Half laughing, half crying, as he mutters inarticulately, holding on to the floating object, slowly recovers self, then:*) Grating—yes—blown off ship—hold on—won't die—won't die . . . (*Gasps, as he sees someone holding onto far side of float*) Ah! Someone—other side—who . . . (*Up, calling, he is very weary*) I say! Over there! Can you hear me?

VOICE (*back, half strangled*). Help!

OFFICER. Voice! I heard . . .

SAILOR (*back as before*). Help!

OFFICER. I hear you! (*Up*) Swim this way! This way! This way!

SAILOR (*in a little closer*). Help!

OFFICER. I can't see you! So dark! This way!

(*Renewed splashing sounds behind.*)

OFFICER. Yes! I see you!

SAILOR. Help me! Help me! I can't . . .

OFFICER. Got you! Hold on! Here!

(*The sailor's exhausted gasping is heard behind.*)

OFFICER. You're all right, man! Don't struggle! You're all right! Both of us all right . . .

SAILOR (*breathing heavily*). Thank you. Thank you.

OFFICER. What did you say? Wait! You . . . You're not one of *our* men.

SAILOR. I—I am—from—submarine.

OFFICER (*in surprise*). Sub . . . (*Down tensely*) By Geoffrey, you *are*! One of *them*!

SAILOR (*in pain*). My—arm . . .

OFFICER. Is it . . . ?

SAILOR. I think . . .

OFFICER. Here—my belt . . . If I can get it off me, I'll tie you on. . . .

SAILOR. No, no, I . . .

OFFICER. Don't be a fool, man! Here—there—over your shoulder . . . There, that does it! How did it happen—to *you*?

SAILOR. The periscope control—something went wrong . . . I was sent up in the conning tower to repair it. All at once there was a great sound, everything went black. I woke up in the water.

OFFICER. By George! Then one of our shots hit you before your torpedo hit *us!* Yes, that's the way it was! A *hit!*

SAILOR. The water is—very cold. . . .

OFFICER (*not quite as vigorously as before*). A hit . . .

SAILOR. It is so dark. . . .

OFFICER. What—what did you say?

SAILOR. Dark . . .

OFFICER. Yes . . . I—I was thinking of . . . I mean, I almost forgot that . . . You, you're all right?

SAILOR. They will not find us. . . .

OFFICER (*sharply*). Why do you say that?

SAILOR. There is no one to find us. . . .

OFFICER. You're out of your head! My ship! (*Down slowly*) You're—out of your—head. . . .

SAILOR (*softly*). I know all my comrades are dead. . . .

OFFICER. Mine. . . .

SAILOR. Would you—talk to me?

OFFICER. Talk?

SAILOR. It would—help me. . . .

OFFICER. You're not very old, are you?

SAILOR. No. . . .

OFFICER. I'm not either, you know. Were—were you from the city?

SAILOR. No—a very small village . . . My father had many milch cows. . . . It is very cold. . . .

OFFICER. You're in pain. Here—I'll help you!

SAILOR. You are good. . . .

OFFICER (*softly*). Aiding and comforting the enemy. . . .

SAILOR. What did you say?

OFFICER. I just thought—you're my enemy. . . .

SAILOR. Am I?

OFFICER. And I'm your enemy. Here, lean against me. . . .

SAILOR. Thank you.

OFFICER. If only the sea would calm down!

SAILOR. Please—tell me—are you—afraid?

OFFICER. I? Are *you?*

SAILOR. Yes!

OFFICER. I am, too. . . .

(*Cracking sound, back.*)

SAILOR (*in alarm*). Wha' . . .

OFFICER (*tensely*). The grating! Wood's breaking up!

SAILOR. What will we . . . ?

OFFICER. Steady! It'll hold together awhile. . . .

SAILOR. But when it . . . ? What will we do?

OFFICER. Swim a little. . . .

SAILOR. I—I . . .

OFFICER. Look! The sky's clearing!

SAILOR. But the water . . .

OFFICER. The stars—bright!

(*Cracking sound, back.*)

SAILOR. It's breaking! I—I . . .

OFFICER. No! Look up! Boy! Look up! It makes it easier!
Look up! There—the bright one! Star of Bethle . . . (*Stops,
then, tensely*) Listen! Tonight! I just remembered! Tonight is Noël!

SAILOR. Noël?

OFFICER. Yes! Yes! Star of Bethlehem—babe in manger—all
the rest of it . . . Noël—don't you understand? *Noël!*

SAILOR. I—am—tired. . . .

(*Cracking sound, back.*)

OFFICER. Ah! Better unfasten your . . . We have to start
swimming for it in a minute!

SAILOR. No. . . .

OFFICER. But . . .

SAILOR. I cannot. . . . My arm . . . I cannot. . . . (*Begins to weep*) You—go . . .

OFFICER. No, no, don't! I'll stay with you. . . .

(*Harp begins, softly behind.*)

SAILOR. You—stay?

OFFICER. Yes—don't be afraid. It'll just be—joining up with our shipmates again. Yes, all of us. There are no enemies— under the sea. . . .

SAILOR. No!

OFFICER. We'll join our friends—together. . . .

(*Harp music rises, water sounds fade slowly. Harp music segues into street sounds. We hear the Santa Claus bell clanging behind.*)

JOE. Ah, nuts, I'm tired ringing! Yeah, what do I have to ring for? The chumps give without ringin'! Wear a red Santa Claus suit and they give!

(*Clink of coins in cup.*)

JOE (*up*). Thank ya, little lady, thank ya! A Merry Christmas to ya! (*Down again*) A dime! Ah, the dumb little kid! Movin' pitchur money, and she gives it to *me!* Ah, the little ones is as dumb as the big ones! Today everybody gives, tomorrow everybody'll take it back! Screwy—yeah, the whole racket! Everybody gives with one hand, but they got the other hand out to get! Yeah, give with one hand and take with the other! Everybody on the make! All over the world! Everybody tryin' to get somethin'! (*Board fade*) Yeah, everybody tryin' to get somethin'! All over the world —tryin' to get somethin'!

(*Board fade-in harp strains, segue into sound of shovel digging into earth, fading back slowly behind.*)

ERIC. Look, look, Cath—they're having a hard time digging tonight. The ground is so hard. Maybe I ought to go help . . . ?

CATH (*sharply*). Eric, no!

ERIC. But, Cath . . .

CATH. No, no, I don't want you to! Come away! I don't want to look any more. Every night it's . . . Come away, Eric!

ERIC (*soothingly*). All right, dear, all right!

CATH. I—I think I want to sit down. . . .

ERIC (*in quick alarm*). Cath, you're not well! You . . .

CATH. No, no, I'm all right. (*As she sits down*) Ah . . . (*Down*) Sit next to me, Eric.

ERIC. All right. . . .

CATH. It's just that—every night—I see that dying and burying is easier than being born. . . .

ERIC. Darling, don't!

CATH. Eric, we've *got* to talk! We've shut our mouths so long —but what good is it? It's happened, and it's happening, and not talking about it doesn't help. It doesn't—it doesn't . . .

ERIC. Cath, please!

CATH (*going right on*). No, I've started to talk, and I'm going to keep on talking! I can't stay sane not talking! We haven't been sane, no, we haven't, Eric!

ERIC. What are you . . . ?

CATH. People who shut their eyes to what's happening to them, and try to make out it's not happening at the very time it's going on, aren't sane, Eric!

ERIC. Oh, darling. . . .

CATH. They aren't and that's the way we've been! All these weeks we've been pretending that nothing's happened! But pretending's got to stop some time, Eric! Now's the time!

Look at us! What are we? What have we got? No home, no friends, no country . . . We sit on the bare ground like animals. No one wants us. No one thinks of us. Two live animals, and there's something alive in me, but I won't live any more like this I tell you! (*Breaks down*) I won't! I won't! (*Cries.*)

ERIC (*soothingly*). Oh, my baby! Cathy! No, don't, baby!

CATH (*tearfully*). We've got to fight, Eric. If we're just animals like *they* say we are, let's fight to live!

ERIC. Fight? No, it's too late to fight. . . .

CATH. Then what? *What?*

ERIC (*down, intensely*). I—don't—*know!*

(*Very soft wind.*)

CATH. Starting—to snow. . . .

ERIC. Yes. . . .

CATH. I wonder if it's warm—under the ground. . . .

ERIC (*aghast*). Cath!

CATH (*flatly, defeatedly*). Why not talk about that, too? Every night we see someone put under the ground. We're the same as they are. Why not talk about it . . . ?

ERIC (*bitterly*). What good am I to you?

CATH (*simply*). That's not right, Eric. We're good for each other, but there's no place above the ground for us. . . .

(*Wind very softly.*)

CATH. I'm right—you know I am. . . .

ERIC (*with difficulty*). What—do you—want to do?

CATH. *You* say it, Eric. . . .

ERIC. I never thought. . . .

CATH. We never thought many things—that some winter's night we'd sit on the ground between two countries and have nothing left but the thought of—being under the ground. . . .

(*Wind sighs.*)

NAHUM (*back*). I beg your pardon. . . .

(CATH *gasps.*)

ERIC (*quickly*). Who is it?

NAHUM (*fade-in full*). I am sorry if I frightened you. . . .

ERIC. What do you want?

NAHUM. Want? To talk a little maybe . . . (*Jewish, quiet, weary, old man in his sixties*) Let me introduce myself. My name—have any of us names here? Does your name matter to me? Does my name matter to you? No! We are how many? A hundred—a hundred and fifty—so many new ones here each day it's hard to keep the number in the head. But we're here because we've committed a crime against society. Yes—all criminals—men and women and children—criminals. So the name doesn't matter—it's the crime. So you don't have to tell me your crime. I know. You, young man, I see it in your face—you have committed the crime of being an intellectual in a society where to think with the head is a danger that must be wiped out for the good of the State. My crime? My crime is quite apparent.

ERIC. What do you want of us?

NAHUM (*slowly*). Want?

ERIC. I'm sorry. . . .

CATH. Are you—alone?

NAHUM. No. I, too, have a wife. She is sleeping. I am a very fortunate man. We have a tent. You—haven't?

ERIC. No. . . .

NAHUM. Soon maybe you won't need one?

CATH. Why do you say that?

NAHUM. There are fortunate people who have friends, relations in countries where there remains some small particle of sanity. It is possible with such friends to get a visa. It is possible that soon both you young people will be so fortunate as to be some place where you will have rest and quiet and welcome.

ERIC. It is possible. . . .

NAHUM. Oh! That is fine! Yes! I—I saw you two sitting here so unhappy, I thought . . . Oh, but if you are going to get a visa, that is fine! I know what a joy it is! Nobody here knows, but only yesterday it came for me! Yes, a visa! On the new quota! My friends in New York! Such wonderful friends! Everything arranged. My wife—I—the next quota . . . Ah, it makes such living easier, eh, my friends! (*Eagerly*) Now—now, tell me—to where are you getting a visa? (*Wind sighs*) You do not answer. Why not? To be free of the hate around us, to know there is somewhere a place for us, that is a joy I want to know—to share the—the thought of with you! So, please, tell me—where are you going from *here*? (*Wind sighs*) You look on me with such cold faces. What have I said?

CATH (*quietly, tensely*). You asked us where are we going from here. . . .

ERIC. Cath, don't . . .

CATH. No, let me tell him! I want him to know where we're going! A visa to another place . . . Yes—we've got a visa!

NAHUM. Good! Good! What country?

CATH. There're no quotas there, not even a single small restriction.

NAHUM. Eh?

CATH (*going right on*). You don't have to have friends or relatives with money. No questions asked or answers given. It doesn't matter what your politics or blood or pocketbook —everybody welcome—welcome and stay until eternity!

NAHUM. You—you're making jokes! Where—where is this visa—passport—whatever it is you're saying? Where is it?

CATH. There!

NAHUM. Huh?

CATH. Yes, there where I'm pointing! Leaning against that fence!

NAHUM (*aghast*). A—a shovel! (*Wind sighs softly*) You—young man—what she says . . .

ERIC (*flatly*). Why not?

NAHUM. But—but you're so young! So—so full of life!

CATH. And no place to live it . . .

NAHUM. But there is hope—from a friend, a relative—a visa?

CATH. No. . . .

NAHUM. But everyone has people somewhere!

ERIC. No one. . . .

NAHUM. I have asked so much. I will ask this: who . . . ?

ERIC. We're tired, old man. Let us alone.

NAHUM. No, please—*who?*

ERIC. All right. Eric Bern. Good night.

NAHUM. Bern? Eric *Bern?*

ERIC. Good night. . . .

NAHUM. Yes! You are! I know it! I have seen your work—oh, many, many times!

CATH. Good night, old man.

NAHUM. No, no, do not send me away! I—I must talk to you! For thousands and thousands of years there have been plain people like me, and we live and we die and what are we? Old stones in the graveyard! But people like you, my friend—every moment of your life is important!

ERIC. Yeah.

NAHUM. Not to yourself—that is why you are a real artist—but important to the rest of us! You give us—how shall I say it?—a piece of beauty that, when men look on it, for a few minutes they are better than men. Or maybe for a few minutes they are like all men will some day *be!* It is important you live! People like you *must* live! While you live, you—you are the conscience of the earth! Live—live long—live and believe the things that brought you to this! Even if you have nothing, live! (*Stops, breathing heavily in his excitement, then:*) All right, all right—I know. It is easy to talk words—but here—here is more . . . Take this —for you . . . use it. It is better for you than for me, who has only left a piece of a life. (*Fade*) Good-bye, good-bye. . . .

ERIC. Old man! What did you give me? Old man! Come back!

CATH. Eric! What did he . . . ?

ERIC. This paper! I don't know . . .

(*Rattle of paper, then:*)

CATH (*tears in voice*). Eric!

ERIC. His—his *visa!*

CATH. Oh, Eric!

ERIC (*dazedly*). Left us his visa!

CATH. We—we can't . . .

ERIC. No, no, of course not!

CATH. Got to find him! Give it back to him!

ERIC. Yes—give back to him. . . .

(*Wind sighs.*)

CATH (*unbelievingly*). Eric—oh, Eric, it can't be true! An old man—stranger—giving us—his life . . . (*Tears*) Oh, Eric!

ERIC. No, darling . . .

CATH. I'm all right. It's just that if there are people like that left in the world—we've got to live, you and I. Just live.

ERIC. Yes . . .

(*Harp music begins far, far back behind.*)

CATH. The sky—clear—how large the stars are!

ERIC. Yes. . . .

CATH. As if this was a special night. Eric, what night *is* it?

ERIC. I—I've lost count.

CATH. It doesn't matter. It's a *good* night. Such a *good* night . . .

(*Harp strains rise, then segue into sound of traffic. Santa bell ringing down behind.*)

JOE. Chumps, chumps, the world's full of chumps! Peace on earth, good will to *who!* Everybody got their mitts out . . . (*Fade*) Everybody wantin' something. Everybody tryin' to do the next guy. . . . Chumps, chumps, all of 'em chumps. . . .

(*The street sounds fade with our cynical Santa Claus, and the harp music rises in the glory of the music of "The Lord's Prayer."*)

POINT OF A GUN

Eight months prior to the writing of these words, I went to the networks. I told them that I was sure that they were as appalled as I was at the indifference with which the Mid-Western and Mid-Eastern parts of our United States were facing the international situation.

I went on to say that it appeared to me that the law of diminishing rights had caught up with speeches and forums; the public was weary of well-intentioned gentlemen pounding the air-waves with threats of dire things to come unless we gave all-out aid to England. The fight, in the last analysis, was our fight.

The answer, I said, was to reach the people through their viscera; give them hard-hitting dramas which would tear their emotions, so that a little good sense could get through the armor-plate which indifference or geographical isolationism had built around them.

My proposal was, specifically, this: I would write and direct a play a week and, would furnish them, equally without fee, a top star of screen or stage to play the lead.

"In other words, gentlemen, I offer you a minimum of $10,000 worth of talent per week for nothing: the best plays I can possibly write, plus Bart Marshall and Bette Davis and Charles Boyer and Olivia de Havilland and Thomas Mitchell and Walter Huston and Martha Scott and dozens of others of our outstanding actors; all we ask in return is a half hour, a half hour which can be of unparalleled influence in shaping public attitudes and so, determining public morals."

As I said, all this took place eight months ago. Both networks were, on the surface, very excited at this opportunity of giving their stations so much talent at no cost to themselves.

But nothing happened!

Never an outright refusal—always: "We are trying to clear the time."

Meanwhile, as the months went by, I heard with terror, and I use the word advisedly, the voices on the air repeating, under the guise of "good old American isolationism," the words which had brought Europe to destruction.

And I saw in the surveys that were being taken how dangerously close to the line of retreat we were, the retreat of do-nothingness which Hitler and Company were using every avenue of insidious propaganda to force us into.

So again and again I went to the networks, pleading for nothing but the right to dramatize not a paean of panic, but plays which would tell through dramatic entertainment what we had, and what we had to be willing to fight for.

I failed to get the time on the air. I failed, not because the officials disagreed with me or with the importance of what had to be done, and not because they doubted that I could do it, but rather because of the intervention of personal ambitions and egos and all of the devilments of the human factor.

Finally, I read somewhere that the Treasury Department was going to put on a full-hour radio program to sell Defense Bonds. I read the prospectus and saw that the program was going to be full of vocalists and comedians, but nowhere along the line was there any mention of dramatization which would effectively arouse the emotions of the listener.

Again I went calling, hat in hand, and at last I was told

I could go ahead and write a play for a name star—whom I was to furnish—and the total time of this complete drama was to be no more than seven minutes!

Point of a Gun *which follows, is one of the plays I did for this Treasury Hour. I was grateful to the gods for the thirteen weeks I had in which to say even the little that could be said in the few moments allotted me—but I couldn't forget the wasted months. . . .*

POINT OF A GUN

OBOLER. I dedicate this, without respect, to those men and women, fortunately few, whose eyes are shut to the grim reality of a wave of the past which may, at any moment, sweep back toward *us*.

MURDOCK (*he is a man in his fifties, very sure of himself; for years he has run a tremendous business successfully, and the "this-is-my-world" attitude is in his voice; at the moment he is in a very good humor at this unexpected visit of a lovely woman*). Well! This is a delightful surprise indeed, Miss Creston! Is the chair comfortable?

CRESTON. Yes.

MURDOCK. A little highball—wine—sherry?

CRESTON. No, thank you.

MURDOCK. You don't mind if I . . .

CRESTON. No, not at all.

(*Sound off slightly, pouring drink, tinkle of bottle against glass, etc.*)

MURDOCK (*off slightly*). Servants' night off . . . I always enjoy it. . . . Like to mix my own drinks. (*Fade-in full, smacks lips, etc.*) Now then, what can I do for you?

CRESTON (*quietly*). Five thousand dollars.

MURDOCK (*blankly*). Wha-at!

CRESTON. Five thousand dollars.

MURDOCK. Five thousand dollars? You—mean a loan?

CRESTON. No.

MURDOCK. Give it to you? (*Chuckles, then suggestively*) Well . . . I see . . .

CRESTON. You don't. It's a matter of business.

MURDOCK. Oh! Well, isn't this entire approach—shall I say— unusual?

CRESTON. Not at all. You have the money—I came to you.

MURDOCK. What is your proposition?

CRESTON. Very simple. You give me five thousand dollars . . .

MURDOCK. And you?

CRESTON. I give you this!

(*Sound of ring being dropped on table.*)

MURDOCK. Why—it's a ring!

CRESTON. Yes.

MURDOCK. But—but it's made out of iron! Why, it isn't **even** worth ten cents!

CRESTON (*firmly*). Five thousand dollars.

MURDOCK (*chuckles*). Did I have the drink or *you?*

CRESTON. Five thousand dollars.

MURDOCK. If it's a joke, I don't understand it.

CRESTON. Do you understand this?

MURDOCK (*sharp intake of breath*). A—gun!

CRESTON. You do understand. . . .

MURDOCK. Young woman, what are you up to?

CRESTON. Five thousand dollars.

MURDOCK. Is it loaded?

CRESTON. Definitely.

MURDOCK. Put it away!

CRESTON. No.

MURDOCK. Are you out of your mind?

CRESTON. Definitely not.

MURDOCK. Miss Creston, I—I've known your family for *years!* Such behavior! Put that gun away and we'll—we'll just for- get all about it!

CRESTON. Five thousand dollars for what I just gave you.

MURDOCK. A piece of worthless metal for five thousand dollars! You're insane!

CRESTON. I'm doing business.

MURDOCK. On whose terms?

CRESTON. On mine. You see, I've got the gun.

MURDOCK. Put it away!

CRESTON. Perhaps I will—after you give me the money.

MURDOCK. If you don't put that gun down, I'll call the police!

CRESTON. And when your butler comes home, he'll call the undertaker.

MURDOCK. You—you . . . (*Laughs forcedly*) Oh, ho! I understand! Oh, yes, I do!

CRESTON. Do you?

MURDOCK. A little joke! Yes, a bet! You've made a bet with your friends—and here you are!

CRESTON (*flatly*). You know it isn't a joke!

MURDOCK (*down*). It's beyond me! A woman of your position . . . Cheap holdup . . .

CRESTON (*tensely*). Don't talk like that or I'll press the trigger!

MURDOCK. No—no . . . I was only saying . . .

CRESTON. Let *me* say it! Your clock on the desk—inside of five minutes you're going to get me the money, or I'll press the trigger.

MURDOCK (*down*). You *are* out of your mind!

CRESTON. Five minutes to do business with me.

MURDOCK. But—but—you're unreasonable! You want my money—and don't give me anything for it. . . .

CRESTON (*interrupting*). I gave you proper value for the money!

MURDOCK. A worthless ring. . . .

CRESTON. It's not worthless, and don't talk so much!

213

MURDOCK (*slowly*). Your eyes . . . I believe—you would . . .

CRESTON. Yes. If you won't do business with me, I'll kill you. . . . One minute from now. . . .

MURDOCK. I'll—get you the money. . . .

CRESTON. No, sit there!

MURDOCK. But how can I get . . . ?

CRESTON. Sit there!

MURDOCK. What . . . ?

CRESTON. You had your chance to do business at my terms! Now I'll get the money myself.

MURDOCK. The—the hammer of the gun . . . Why do you . . . ?

(*Gasping intake of breath.*)

CRESTON. How unfortunate you were unreasonable!

MURDOCK (*barely able to talk*). I! Unreasonable? But I offered—no! Please don't . . . Please . . . I'll give you the money. I won't tell anyone. Put down the gun . . . Come with me . . . I'll never tell the police . . .

CRESTON. You're very frightened, aren't you?

MURDOCK. Don't—press—the—trigger. (*He can hardly speak*) Don't—press—the—trigger!

CRESTON (*after tense pause, calmly*). I won't.

(MURDOCK *gasps.*)

CRESTON. I've done what I wanted to do.

MURDOCK (*hoarsely*). Wha' . . .

CRESTON. Frighten you—horribly. . . .

MURDOCK (*with difficulty*). Why?

CRESTON. Business, as usual.

MURDOCK. What?

CRESTON. I heard you give that speech last night.

MURDOCK. Eh? Wha'—wha' . . .

CRESTON. You still have difficulty in talking. Good! That'll give me a chance. Before you call the police, as I am sure you'll want to do for what I have done to you. Yes, I heard you make a speech last night. You said that you were a businessman, and it wasn't good business, you said, to make everyone angry at us. That if unfortunate things are happening in the world—well, that was just too bad. That you were a businessman, and it was your American privilege to do business as usual with whomever you pleased. That's why I came here tonight.

MURDOCK. I don't understand.

CRESTON. To do business with you the way *they'll* do business with you when *they're* ready to do business with you. *Pointing a gun at you.* . . . No, don't bother saying anything! Let me take you step by step, the way *we* did business tonight. You let me into your home. You took it for granted that I believed in law and order, decency between people—and so you let me into your home. Then I wanted to do business with you—get something *you* had and, in turn, offer you something *I* had. But what *you* had was much more valuable than what *I* had. But that didn't matter. *I was doing business with you at the point of a gun.* When you protested, I told you I was going to—what is the word they use?—yes, "liquidate" you as a very unreasonable fellow. And then, of course, take what I want. It was all quite simple. Because you wanted to do business, within certain degrees, as a civilized gentleman—and I wanted to do business the way *they* will do it, if we take your advice and shut our eyes to the realities of their plans. So, there it is. Tonight I tried to show you realities. Even if the events abroad didn't stir the human decencies in you, self-preservation ought to stir you to want to fight for your way of life—

to fight for a better future of a better sort of "business as usual." You can call the police now.

MURDOCK (*slowly*). No . . . Just go. . . .

CRESTON. Thank you. (*Fade*) Good-bye.

MURDOCK. No, wait!

CRESTON (*back in*). Yes?

MURDOCK. That gun—was it loaded?

CRESTON. You hadn't noticed—it's a very old gun. Look.

MURDOCK. Ah. . . .

CRESTON. My great-grandfather loaded it a long time ago. Before he put it away, he told my grandmother always to see that it was loaded in case that somewhere, sometime in a future generation, someone forgot that liberty wasn't a gift, but a victory!

(*Musical curtain.*)

THIS PRECIOUS FREEDOM

*I hear you crying that the people are indifferent. You say
how can they insist on "business as usual," on "life as usual?"
How can they expect to win without sacrifice?*

*I say that you with your plaint are the fool! For, during
the years when you could have spoken to the people, during
the years when you were saying that Spain was not to our
interest, that Ethiopia was not to our interest, that the cries
of the tortured in Manchukuo and the Third Reich were not
to our interest, you were digging the grave of your own security.*

Raymond Massey and I came to New York to do This
Precious Freedom. *The network thought the play was "dan-
gerous," that it might "arouse" the listening public.*

*Since that is what both Mr. Massey and I wanted above
all else, we fought and we pleaded and we Dale Carnegied
and we traded and we raged until finally they let us do our
broadcast.*

*The play was given the only citation awarded any commer-
cial program by the Institute of Radio meeting at Ohio Uni-
versity.*

*In making the award, the judges, Messrs. Wheatley, Reed
and Cohen stated: "Portrayal of effect on American people of
loss of civil rights, accompanying totalitarian invasion, in
terms of one man's experience. This was the only commercial
program cited by your judges. The author is one of radio's
writers who is fighting the good fight for democracy steadily,
wherever he can."*

*I can add only that as long as there are actors such as Ray-
mond Massey to help one in the good fight, then the pen
writes freely in the hope of a saner world.*

218

THIS PRECIOUS FREEDOM

(*Sound of airplane, down and continuing.*)

JOHN (*he is in a very good mood*). Morgan?

MORGAN (*off slightly*). Yes, sir?

JOHN. Can't you make this crate of mine go faster?

MORGAN. Sorry, Mr. Stevenson. We're bucking a pretty stiff headwind.

JOHN (*chuckles*). Come now—don't tell me the heavens are conspiring to keep me from getting back to work! Open her up, Morgan—I've had enough vacation!

MORGAN. Yes, sir. . . .

(*For a few seconds we hear nothing but the airplane climbing, then, motor down, continuing behind.*)

JOHN. That's better! You know, Morgan, I should think you'd be as eager to get to the city as I am! After all, a young fellow like you—a month up in the woods with nothing around but those overstuffed squaws! (*Chuckles*) Well, I for one am going to be glad to get back in harness again! Of course, I am not going to admit that to Mrs. Stevenson! I talked to her for the last ten years about cutting myself off from civilization and having a real vacation and now . . .

(*Airplane motor begins to miss; continuing to cut in and out intermittently behind.*)

JOHN. Morgan? What's the matter?

MORGAN. Oil-line open!

JOHN. By George!

(*Airplane motor cuts out completely; whine of plane gliding into forced landing.*)

MORGAN. Take it easy, Mr. Stevenson! We're okay! Just fasten your safety belt!

JOHN. But where are you going to land? *Where?*

MORGAN. Field ahead! Hold on! Don't be afraid!

JOHN (*tensely*). Don't be a fool! I've been in forced landings before! All I want to do is get down there—fast! I've got to get to the city! I've got to get back to my business!

(*Whine of plane increases, segue into musical transition.*)

(*Sound of knocking on door.*)

MORGAN. Guess there's no one home, Mr. Stevenson.

JOHN. No one in the fields—no one to help us . . . Fine end to a vacation!

MORGAN. Guess we'd better try to flag a ride into town. No use standing around . . .

JOHN (*sharply*). Wait a minute!

MORGAN. Uh?

JOHN. Someone coming!

(*Door opening back, slowly, squeakily.*)

JOHN. Well! How do you do? We just had a forced landing out on one of your fields and I . . .

FARMER (*interrupting sharply*). What do you want?

JOHN (*affably*). But I'm trying to tell you! We had a forced landing out there in your field! Could I use your telephone? I have a very important engagement. . . .

FARMER (*interrupting gruffly*). Wait a minute! Who are you?

JOHN (*not angrily, but declaratively*). I don't see what earthly difference that makes. After all, all I want is to use your telephone. . . .

FARMER. Go away!

(*Sound of slammed door.*)

JOHN (*amazed*). Why, you . . . (*Then to pilot*) Morgan, did you see that? Slammed the door in my face!

MORGAN (*flatly*). Yeah. . . .

JOHN. In my face! Infernal fool! What could he possibly have been thinking?

MORGAN (*flatly, thoughtfully*). I don't know, Mr. Stevenson. . . . But that guy was awful scared.

(*Musical transition. Wind sighs softly behind.*)

JOHN. This is the main road, isn't it?

MORGAN. That's what the sign says.

JOHN. Then where's the traffic? We've stood here for an hour!

MORGAN. Honest, Mr. Stevenson, I don't know from nothin'!

JOHN. Yes. I'm beginning to think that if you'd spent more time, before we took off, getting that engine in condition and less time . . .

(*Begin to fade-in sound of truck approaching down road.*)

MORGAN. Wait, Mr. Stevenson! Here comes a truck!

JOHN. Well! About time!

MORGAN. If he don't stop . . .

JOHN. We'll make him stop! (*Up*) Driver! Driver! Stop! (*Etc., ad lib.*)

(MORGAN *joins in.*)

(*Truck pulls in close, stops with squeal of brakes.*)

JOHN (*up*). Driver—my plane . . . I had a forced landing out here! Could you drive me into the city? (*Pause*) Did you hear me? I said, could you drive me into the city. I'll give you twenty-five dollars!

DRIVER (*off slightly*). Okay! Jump in!

JOHN. Morgan, you'd better stay here with the plane. I'll send someone back.

MORGAN. Yes, sir.

JOHN (*with effort as he pulls himself up into truck*). Ah!
(*Bring in sound of engine*) I hope you're a fast driver!

DRIVER (*in full*). Fast enough. . . .

(*Gears—truck starting off.*)

JOHN (*calling back*). Stay with the plane, Morgan!

MORGAN (*back, fading fast*). Right!

(*Sound of truck down and continuing back behind.*)

JOHN. Well! For a while there I thought there weren't any
trucks on the road any more!

DRIVER (*flatly*). Not many. . . .

JOHN. But this is the main highway—now it's practically
empty! Why?

DRIVER. Mister, I'm just a driver!

JOHN. Oh! Some sort of labor disturbance, eh?

DRIVER (*slowly*). You kiddin' me?

JOHN. What're you talking about?

DRIVER. I'm not talkin', mister—you are. . . .

JOHN. Look here, I've been vacationing up in the north woods
for weeks. I deliberately haven't read a newspaper or heard
a radio in all that time! But now that I'm back—well, I
might as well start taking it again. What's up? Well, why
don't you answer me?

DRIVER. Mister, I'm just drivin'.

JOHN (*irritably*). What is this, anyway? All I want is a civil
answer!

DRIVER (*flatly*). I don't know any answers, mister. You'll find
them out for yourself.

(*Bring up sound of truck, segue into musical transition.*)

(*Sound of city streets down and continuing behind.*)

JOHN (*counting out money*). Fifteen—twenty—twenty-five!
There you are!

DRIVER. Okay!

JOHN. Well, I certainly didn't get any conversation for my money!

DRIVER. Are you gettin' off, mister?

JOHN. Yes—of course. (*Dryly*) Huh—*manners* certainly haven't improved while I've been away! Good-bye!

(*Sound of truck door opening and closing; sound of truck moving away; bring up sound of city street slightly.*)

NEWSBOY (*off slightly*). Paper? Paper, mister? Paper?

JOHN. Yes! Yes, of course, boy! Let me have one of each!

NEWSBOY. Huh?

JOHN. I said one of each—each newspaper!

NEWSBOY (*glumly*). Who ya kiddin'?

JOHN. Say, what's come over everyone? Here—give me a *Tribune*—a *News*—*Times*—all of them! Well, don't stand there! I'm in a hurry!

NEWSBOY (*down, tensely*). Mister, don't you know?

JOHN. Know what? *What?* (*Up, calling after him*) Boy! Boy, where are you going? Boy, come back here!

(*Musical transition.*)

ELEVATOR MAN. Goin' up.

JOHN (*fading-in fast*). Yes! Take me upstairs! Fast!

(*Sound of elevator door closing; elevator whine beginning and continuing behind.*)

ELEVATOR MAN. What floor?

JOHN. Well! I have been away too long! (*Seeing who it is*) Oh! Where's Tom?

ELEVATOR MAN (*flatly*). He ain't here.

JOHN. Yes, but *where* is he? Well? Didn't you hear me? Where is he?

(*Elevator coming to stop, door pulled back.*)

ELEVATOR MAN. Here's your floor, mister.

JOHN. By George, I've had enough of this nonsense! Ever

since I got off the plane . . . (*Sound of closing elevator door*) Don't close that door! What! Well, of all the . . . Well, I certainly won't stand for *that!* Building manager's going to hear about *him!* Get to office—phone him . . . (*Sound of his footsteps along hallway, behind.*)

JOHN (*stream of consciousness*). Well! At least office is still here! (*Sound of his trying door. Stream of consciousness*) Door stuck . . . (*Sound of trying door again*) Fine business! Can't even get into own office! (*Sounds of effort as he tries door*) Well! (*Sound of knocking on glass panel of door*) Open up! Open up! No one in there! Door must be locked! Where's my key? Nice business! Eleven-thirty and they haven't even opened the office! (*Rattle of keys, key in lock of door, etc., behind*) That's loyalty for you! Didn't expect me back so soon, I suppose! (*Sound of door opening*) Entire office staff decided to take a vacation while . . . (*Breaks off short as he sees that office is empty*) What, in the . . . ! (*Sound of hurried footsteps as he walks across echoing office to another door, opens door. Aghast*) Desk— files—gone! Office empty! Where, in the . . . ? Where . . . ?

REGAN (*back slightly*). Are ya lookin' for somethin', mister?

JOHN. Wha' . . . Regan!

REGAN. Huh? (*Fading-in full*) Who are you?

JOHN. Regan! Don't you know me? What's going on here?

REGAN (*stuttering*). M-Mr. Stevenson!

JOHN. What's happened to my office? Where are all my things? What's going on here? Don't stand there with your mouth open! Tell me!

REGAN. Dead . . . I—I thought you were dead!

JOHN. What are you talking about? Everyone knew I was going on a vacation! What's happened to my things? Where are all my people? Answer me!

Here DKle.

REGAN. You—you don't know?

JOHN. Know what? Talk words, man! What's happened to my business?

REGAN (*softly, frightenedly*). M-Mr. Stevenson, I—I can't tell you. . . .

JOHN. What do you mean you can't tell me? You're the manager of the building! Who moved out my office? Where are all my things? *Answer me!*

REGAN (*half-choked*). You're hurting me!

JOHN. Answer me!

REGAN. You—can't *ask* questions, Mr. Stevenson. . . .

JOHN. Wha' . . .

REGAN. Go home, Mr. Stevenson! Please—go home—*quick!*

(*Musical transition.*)

(*We hear* JOHN'S *heavy breathing together with sound of his running up short flight of stone steps; sound at head of steps, key in lock, opening and closing door.*)

JOHN (*calling*). Jean! Jean! (*Sound of his running across floor, trying another door*) Jean! Where are you? Jean! (*Up*) Jean!

VOICE No. 1 (*off slightly*). Lookin' for somebody, fella?

JOHN (*startled*). Who . . . ?

VOICE No. 1. Stand still! Frisk him, Joe.

VOICE No. 2. Yeah. . . .

JOHN. Who in the devil . . . ?

VOICE No. 1. Keep your mouth shut!

JOHN. How dare you! Get out of my house!

VOICE No. 1. Start walkin', fella!

JOHN. Walking? What do you mean?

VOICE No. 1. Somebody wants to talk to you.

JOHN. W-what are you? Police?

VOICE No. 2. Sure! Start movin'!

JOHN. But—but why?

VOICE No. 1. Mister, get goin'!

JOHN. No! If you're police, where are your warrants? Yes, where're your warrants?

VOICE No. 1. Here!

JOHN. No, don' . . . (*Voice cuts off sharply with thud of gun against head, followed by thud of body on floor.*)

(*Musical transition.*)

JOHN (*in close, groans as he recovers*). Ahh . . . Head . . . (*Groans again*) Room . . . Where . . . ? What . . . ? (*Sound of door, back, footsteps fading in across floor*) Old man . . . What does he . . . ?

(*Footsteps in close, stop.*)

OLD MAN (*whispers hoarsely*). You all right?

JOHN. Yes . . . (*Groans.*)

OLD MAN. No! You better not try to stand up! Take it easy!

JOHN (*with effort*). Are they police?

OLD MAN. Yeah—in a way. . . .

JOHN (*still dazed*). Mistake . . . Someone's made a mistake. . . .

OLD MAN. No—no mistake, Mr. Stevenson . . .

JOHN. My name—you know it . . .

OLD MAN. Yeah. I used to do business with your company once. . . . Always treated me fine . . .

JOHN. Who—are—you?

OLD MAN. Me? Nobody. Just sort of clean up. . . .

JOHN. Where am I?

OLD MAN. Mr. Stevenson, there are some things I can't tell you.

JOHN. Mistake—horrible mistake. I'm John Stevenson. I—I'm a respectable citizen. I . . . (*Suddenly realizing*) My wife!

Got to get in touch with Jean. She'll be worried . . . Wasn't home . . . She . . .

OLD MAN. Now take it easy, Mr. Stevenson!

JOHN (*building*). No, wait! The mayor! Yes, the mayor! He's a friend of mine! Got to get to the telephone! Tell the mayor what's happened!

OLD MAN (*hastily, through above*). No, Mr. Stevenson! Please keep your voice down! If they come in here again . . .

JOHN. Let them come in! I've got nothing to be afraid of! I've done nothing! Come into my house without a warrant . . . They've got no right!

OLD MAN. Mr. Stevenson, you don't understand! Please, Mr. Stevenson!

JOHN. Understand *what?* Tell me!

OLD MAN (*slowly*). Things are—different. . . .

JOHN. Different? What do you mean? What's it got to do with *this*—with me?

OLD MAN. Mr. Stevenson, somethin' I don't understand . . . Where've you been?

JOHN. Been? Out of the city—up north in the woods! Don't waste time, man! Call up the mayor! Tell him . . .

OLD MAN. But that won't do any good!

JOHN. Why not? There's been a mistake. . . .

OLD MAN. But there's *been* no mistake, Mr. Stevenson! Please listen to me—please! I seen lots of things happen here the last couple of weeks, but I—I didn't know any of them, so it didn't matter! But I know *you*, kind of, so I'll tell *you!*

JOHN. Tell me *what?*

OLD MAN. It's about . . . Well, I guess maybe you're the only one in the whole country don't know about it.

JOHN. Talk sense, man!

OLD MAN. I'm tryin' to! I—I don't know exactly how to say it. You see, I never had much learnin', so maybe the words won't be right, but I'll try to give you the idea.

JOHN (*impatiently*). Well? *Well?*

OLD MAN. First, they, well, that part of the Constitution—they threw it out!

JOHN (*blankly*). Part of the—what the devil are you talking about?

OLD MAN. The part of the Constitution—you know—about rights. Threw it out! The way I've got it figured out, when the others ganged up on us—all them battleships and airplanes—well, there wasn't much we could do now, was there? Had to sort of—well, throw in the towel.

JOHN (*pause, then*). Are you trying to tell me that while I was away there has been an *invasion?*

OLD MAN. Invasion? Well, they ain't gone all the way. . . . I mean, just this piece of the coast, but here they're runnin' things the way they want them to be run. And, mister, it's only been two weeks, but if I was to tell you all that . . .

JOHN (*furiously, interrupting*). Get out of here!

OLD MAN. Wha' . . .

JOHN. You heard me! Get out! Haven't I had enough today without listening to you, you crazy old fool?

OLD MAN. But, Mr. Stevenson, I . . .

JOHN (*furiously*). Get out, I tell you! (*Up*) Listen—someone out there! Get this crazy old fool out of here! If this is a jail, get me my lawyer! (*Board fade*) What am I being held for? What are the charges? Get me my lawyer! Get me my lawyer!

(*Musical transition, cross fade with above fade.*)

EXAMINER (*he has a cold precise voice*). So you insist on having a lawyer?

228

JOHN. Certainly! It's my right!

EXAMINER. Is it?

JOHN. You know mighty well it is! If there's some criminal charge against me, I have a right to have a lawyer!

EXAMINER (*his coldness breaking up, furiously*). Right—right —right! What *right* are you talking about?

JOHN (*very quietly, holding himself in control*). You're obviously some sort of police official, and very obviously think you're doing your duty. Well, let me tell you, a horrible mistake has been made. I'm no criminal. I'm John Stevenson—an ordinary businessman. Call Mayor Alden—he'll tell you.

EXAMINER. He'll tell us nothing. The man is of no importance!

JOHN. No import— But the mayor . . .

EXAMINER. Mayor of *what*? (*Chuckles*) The worms?

JOHN (*blankly*). Worms. . . .

EXAMINER. The man is dead. . . .

JOHN. Oh. . . .

EXAMINER. But that, too, is of no importance. What is important to me is you—and your activities.

JOHN. I—I don't know what you're talking about!

EXAMINER. That is not very clever, believe me.

JOHN (*wearily*). I don't know what you're talking about!

EXAMINER. Your so-called vacation trip. (*Sharply*) Whom did you meet?

JOHN. Meet? What do you . . . ?

EXAMINER (*interrupting sharply*). Don't *ask* questions! *Answer* them! You have been out of the city for weeks! Suddenly, you return! Where were you?

JOHN. On—on my vacation, of course! Is there any law against *that*?

EXAMINER. For the last time, don't try to be clever with me!

JOHN (*wearily*). Once and for all, will you tell me what the charges are against me? There's been some kind of terrible mistake—all right. But tell me what the charges are! Give me a chance to clear myself!

EXAMINER (*tensely quiet*). I have wasted quite enough time with you, Stevenson. . . .

JOHN. Let me post bond. . . . Let me call my lawyer. . . . You've no right to keep me here! My wife—she wasn't home when I was taken away. . . . She'll be worried. . . . She . . .

EXAMINER (*interrupting*). Yes! Yes! Of course, your wife! Have you any idea where your wife is, Mr. Stevenson?

JOHN. Why—why, home, I suppose! Yes, she must be there now! If you'll hand me the phone . . .

EXAMINER. She is *not* home—believe me!

JOHN. Why do you say that?

EXAMINER (*up*). All right, sergeant!

(*Door opening.*)

VOICE (*far back*). In there!

JOHN (*in surprise*). Jean! Jean!

(JEAN *in fast, weeping.*)

JOHN. Jean, what are you doing here? What is it? Jean, stop crying! I'm all right! There's been some crazy mistake, but . . . (*Slowly*) Jean, why should you cry like this? You never cry. (*Sharply*) Jean! The children! Are they all right? Jean, talk to me! Stop crying and talk to me!

EXAMINER. She knows better. . . .

JOHN (*turning on him furiously*). Better? What are you talking about? Jean, lift your face! What happened? What's wrong?

EXAMINER. Take her away!

JOHN. No! She'll stay here. . . . Jean, *you* tell me what this is about! Has everyone gone crazy! What . . . ? (*Sounds of scuffling together with:*) No, let go of her! You blasted . . . !
(JEAN *calls his name, cut off by closing door.*)

JOHN (*fighting them*). Let go of me! Bring her back here! Bring her back here! I'll kill you! I'll . . . Jean (*Up*) Jean!
(*Musical transition.*)

EXAMINER (*very calmly, very precisely, almost like professor giving lecture*). You will be quite calm now, eh, Mr. Stevenson? Yes, I am sure you will. . . . We have quite a technic for calming down unreasonable people, haven't we?

JOHN (*with effort; from his voice all that he has gone through in the intervening time is obvious*). You—you . . . !

EXAMINER. So you still persist in talking. . . . (*Sound of slap of open hand against face*) So . . . Discipline—that is the first lesson you must learn in this new state of ours! Discipline! Always discipline! It is very strange, Mr. Stevenson. You have been here now over an hour, and yet there is very little fear in your face. . . . I wonder why? Astonishment—yes—a sort of astonished wonder in your face, as if you can't believe . . . (*Slowly*) Could you *possibly* be ignorant of the facts? This glorious new state that we are planting here! This fulfillment of the dream some of us have had since the day we heard a voice telling us of our destiny! A dream that will come true! This will soon be our nation now, Mr. Stevenson—*ours*—all of it! Your men are fighting, yes, but we will win! Wonder in your face . . . Yes—sometimes even *I* ask myself, can it be true? The wonder of it—and yet, no wonder of it! The plan, Mr. Stevenson—the plan . . . Always it was there, and always we followed it! We poured our propaganda in on you—yes, we used your own weaknesses against you! We cried out, "Let us speak! It is our right!" How simple it was to use your rights against you! So now you have no rights, Stevenson . . . (*Building vaingloriously*) *No* one has rights but *we* who are the lead-ers! (*He recovers himself, resumes his quiet, studied manner*) I was quite carried away, wasn't I? I must not forget to let *you* speak. (*Quickly, tensely*) We want to know many things: every detail of your airplane trip, whom you saw, which of our enemies are hiding up there where you were! I warn you—speak quickly, Stevenson! Who are your friends? Which of our enemies did you meet? (*Fade*) Who were your friends? Whom did you meet? Where did you go? Whom did you meet? Where did you go? Whom did you meet? Where? Why?

(*Musical transition. Cross fade with above fade.*)

VOICE No. 1 (*with effort. They are carrying Stevenson's body*). Put him here. . . .

VOICE No. 2. Yeah. . . .

(*Thud of body being dropped on floor.*)

VOICE No. 2. Dead yet?

VOICE No. 1. No, not yet. . . .

(*Sneak music in, and continue far back behind.*)

JOHN (*in close, semi-monotone of stream of consciousness thoughts in his mind, disjointed, dazed; the man is half dead*). Dead yet . . . Who said that? Can't see . . . All mixed up . . . Vacation . . . Enemies of the State . . . Airplane . . . I don't know . . . All mixed up . . . (*Begins to cry, then*) No . . . Got to stop . . . Got to think . . . (*In pain*) Pain . . . No . . . Got to think things out . . . What's happened to me . . . ? What . . . ?

VOICE No. 1 (*whispering, in close*). Our glorious new State!

VOICE No. 2. We who are leaders!

Voice No. 1. This will be *our* nation soon!

John (*stream of consciousness*). Voices in my head . . . All mixed up . . . Think things out . . . Got to . . . Go crazy! From the start . . . Yes, from the start . . . Vacation . . . Coming back from my vacation . . .

(*Sound of airplane gliding in, out quickly behind.*)

John. Yes—landed plane. . . .

Farmer (*whispers*). Go away! (*Fading*) Go away!

John. Yes! That farmer!

Morgan (*whispering*). That guy was awful scared! (*Fade*) Awful scared!

John. Yes. Morgan, you *did* say that!

Truck Driver (*whispering*). I don't know any answers. (*Fade*) You'll find them out for yourself. . . .

John. Yes! Truck driver!

Newsboy. Mister, don't you know? (*Fade*) Mister, don't you know?

John. Yes! Newsboy! He, too!

Regan (*whispering*). You can't ask questions, Mr. Stevenson!

Old Man. Things are different. . . .

Regan (*fading*). You can't ask questions, Mr. Stevenson!

Old Man (*fading far back*). Things are different, Mr. Stevenson. . . .

John (*on cue through above*). Yes, yes, they said that! Everyone said that! Everyone talking to me! Trying to tell me! I didn't know! I *don't* know!

Examiner (*whispering*). This will soon be our nation now!

John. No! It isn't true! It's all in my head! Jean! Jean, where are you? Jean, where are the children? *Jean!* (*Down, tensely*) Did I—just cry out? Cry out? Why should I cry out? (*Flatly, declaratively*) My name is John Stevenson.

233

. . . I have a business in the Central Building. . . . I have a house on Arcade Street. . . . I have a wife, two children— a boy and a girl. . . . We have a good life. . . . A good life. . . .

VOICE NO. 2. Is he dead?

VOICE NO. 1. Not yet. . . .

VOICE NO. 2 (*fading*). Dead? Dead? Dead?

JOHN. Why do I keep thinking that? Who said it to me?

VOICE NO. 2 (*fade-in and fade-out fast*). Dead? Dead? Dead?

JOHN (*calmly now, full possession of faculties*). Yes—I know . . . I remember . . . Going to kill me . . . I'm an enemy of the State!

EXAMINER (*whispering*). Our glorious new state!

JOHN. But it's so funny! John Stevenson—832 Arcade Street— enemy of the State! I went on a vacation. . . . I came home —and I'm an enemy of the State! Yes—my wife—the chil- dren—that's what he said—everyone enemies of the new State! (*Tensely*) No! It's madness! I'm me . . . I can do what I want. I can get up out of here! Yes, I *will* get out of here! I'm John Stevenson! You've hurt me! There's blood . . . (*Building*) No, I *will* get out of here! You can't accuse me and not give me a trial! You can't come into my house! You can't take away my business! I'm a free man! I'm an *American!*

EXAMINER (*whispering*). This will be our nation soon. . . . (*Fade*) Ours—ours—ours!

JOHN (*down again, slowly*). But how could that be?

OLD MAN (*whispering*). Seein' as we weren't ready (*Fade*) there wasn't much we could do, now, was there?

VOICE NO. 1 (*whispering back*). Let's mind our own busi- ness! Nothing to do with us!

JOHN. Who—who said that?

234

VOICE No. 1 (*whispering in close*). Let's mind our own business. . . . Nothing to do with us. . . .

JOHN (*slowly*). I remember, *I* said that! Yes, all the time—*I* said that!

VOICE No. 2 (*echo*). Men have no rights!

JOHN. None of my business?

VOICE No. 2 (*echo*). We spit on freedom!

JOHN. None of my business?

VOICE No. 2 (*echo*). Might is right!

JOHN. None of my business?

VOICE No. 2 (*echo*). Our Leader—our people—our world!

JOHN. None of my business? How could I . . . ? Why did I . . . ?

VOICES (*whispering fast*). Don't antagonize them! We'll have to do business with them! Let them talk! Mind our own business! Don't antagonize them! (*Etc., fading.*)

JOHN. Yes—all the things I said!

OLD MAN (*whispering*). There really wasn't much we could do, now, was there?

EXAMINER (*echo*). Our glorious new State!

VOICE No. 2 (*whispering*). Dead yet? He will be! Dead yet? He will be! (*Fade*) Dead yet? He will be!

JOHN (*slowly*). I *do* understand now. . . . I wanted everything, and I . . . didn't want to risk anything to keep what I had. . . . What I had . . . (*Tensely*) *What I had* . . .

VOICES. Your home is your kingdom. . . .
    Your own god is *your* god. . . .
    Say what you want to say. . . .
    Write what you want to write. . . .
    (*Fading out*) Trial by jury. . . .
    Sanctity of person. . . .
    Due process of law. . . .

JOHN (*brokenly*). *What I had* . . .

JEAN (*calling*). John!

JOHN (*growing weaker*). Jean! Is that you? No. . . . In my head . . . So dark . . . There's blood in my . . . So dark . . .

VOICE NO. 2. Dead yet? He will be. (*Fade*) Dead yet? He will be.

JOHN. Jean, I'll tell you something very funny—I'm not afraid to die. . . . No . . . I'm afraid to go on living. If all this isn't really a dream—bad dream—then I don't want to go on living. Everywhere I'd turn, they'd be there.

VOICES. Shut your mouth!

You can't do that!

Come with us!

We accuse you of . . . !

Shut your mouth!

Give us that!

Keep moving!

Attention!

Shut your mouth!

Shut your mouth!

(VOICES *cut off knife-clean with:*)

JOHN (*sharply*). No! I can't live with *that!* All my life I lived with freedom! Jean, we didn't know it was freedom, did we? Living in our house—a good life—our neighbors—not hating anybody—and—and driving in the country with the kids wherever we wanted to go—and feeling sure of the future for the kids, because whatever was wrong here we, ourselves, could fix with work and with our votes and with what we knew was right in our hearts. I never said, *"This* is freedom!" But it *was!* It *was!* When they talked to me about losing it, I said, "Don't be fools! No one'll take it

from us!" I thought freedom was like the air—always with me as long as I lived! I thought I didn't have to do anything about it! Jean, I was wrong! I—I've got the words now to say it! What I had wasn't a *gift*—it was a *victory!* And I can't live without it! (*Building*) Do you hear me out there? I can't live without it! To *say* what I think is right —to *do* what I think is right! That's the only life I want! It *is* life! I'll live for it! I'll fight for it! (*Up, vibrantly*) *This precious freedom!*
(*Musical curtain.*)

GLOSSARY OF RADIO TERMS

BACK: Dialogue or effect is off-microphone, in other words, not at full volume in relation to other speeches or effects.

CONTINUING BACK BEHIND: The particular effect fades back, but continues in background of scene.

CROSS-FADE: One sound or musical effect decreases in volume as another effect increases in volume.

CUT: Music or dialogue or effect stops abruptly; also used to indicate necessity of cutting material because of time limitations.

ECHO CHAMBER: Device used to give voice or music resonance to illustrate, for example, that action takes place in large hall.

FADE-IN: Gradual increase of volume.

FADE-OUT: Gradual decrease of volume.

FILTER: Device used to change quality of voice to indicate, for example, that person is speaking on telephone.

MOOD MUSIC: Music as background to plant mood of scene.

MUSICAL CURTAIN: Music used at end of play as tag or curtain.

MUSIC (OR SOUND) UP: Rise in volume.

MUSIC (OR SOUND) DOWN: Decrease of volume.

ON-MIKE: Close to microphone; full level.

SEGUE: One effect blends into the other.

SOUND (OR MUSIC) OUT: Sound or musical effect stops.

STREAM OF CONSCIOUSNESS: Thoughts in mind of character; method of delivery should be quiet, semi-monotone, with far less coloring than "conscious" speeches.

STREAM OF CONSCIOUSNESS MUSIC: A musical theme used recurringly to indicate that dialogue is in mind of character.

TRANSITIONAL MUSIC: Music used as bridge between scenes.